Pearson Revise

Pearson Edexcel GCSE (9-1)

History

Spain and the 'New World', c1490–1555

Revision Guide and Workbook

Series Consultant: Harry Smith
Author: Brian Dowse

A note from the publisher

In order to ensure that this resource offers high-quality support for the associated Pearson qualification, it has been through a review process by the awarding body. This process confirms that this resource fully covers the teaching and learning content of the specification or part of a specification at which it is aimed. It also confirms that it demonstrates an appropriate balance between the development of subject skills, knowledge and understanding, in addition to preparation for assessment.

Endorsement does not cover any guidance on assessment activities or processes (e.g. practise questions or advice on how to answer assessment questions), included in the resource nor does it prescribe any particular approach to the teaching or delivery of a related course.

While the publishers have made every attempt to ensure that advice on the qualification and its assessment is accurate, the official specification and associated assessment guidance materials are the only authoritative source of information and should always be referred to for definitive guidance.

Pearson examiners have not contributed to any sections in this resource relevant to examination papers for which they have responsibility.

Examiners will not use endorsed resources as a source of material for any assessment set by Pearson.

Endorsement of a resource does not mean that the resource is required to achieve this Pearson qualification, nor does it mean that it is the only suitable material available to support the qualification, and any resource lists produced by the awarding body shall include this and other appropriate resources.

For the full range of Pearson revision titles across KS2, 11+, KS3, GCSE, Functional Skills, AS/A Level and BTEC visit:
www.pearsonschools.co.uk/revise

Contents

SUBJECT CONTENT

Spain reaches the 'New World', c1490–1512

Spanish exploration
1. Spain, c1490
2. Columbus and sponsorship
3. Columbus's first voyage, 1492

Columbus and the Caribbean
4. The Bahamas and the Caribbean
5. Impact of contact with natives
6. Rivalry with Portugal

Spanish claims
7. Columbus's other voyages
8. Effects of Spanish settlement
9. Development of an imperial policy

The conquistadors, 1513–c1528

Start of an empire
10. Balboa and the conquistadors, 1513–28
11. The conquest of Cuba
12. The voyage of Magellan

Conquest of Mexico
13. Expedition to Mexico, 1519
14. Key events of the conquest

Spain's impact
15. Cortes's actions 1523–28
16. Consequences for the Aztecs
17. Pizarro and Panama

The Spanish Empire, c1528–c1555

Conquest of the Incas
18. Pizarro's arrival in Peru
19. Pizarro's conquest of Peru

Expansion of empire
20. Discovery of silver in Bolivia and Mexico
21. Governing the empire
22. The foundation of La Paz, 1548

Impact of the New World
23. Silver and gold
24. The impact of trade
25. The government of the New World

SKILLS
26. Exam overview
27. Question 1: Explaining consequences 1
28. Question 1: Explaining consequences 2
29. Question 2: Analytical narrative 1
30. Question 2: Analytical narrative 2
31. Question 3: Explaining importance 1
32. Question 3: Explaining importance 2

33. PRACTICE

43. ANSWERS

A small bit of small print

Pearson Edexcel publishes Sample Assessment Material and the Specification on its website. This is the official content and this book should be used in conjunction with it. The questions in *Now try this* have been written to help you practise every topic in the book. Remember: the real exam questions may not look like this.

Had a look ☐　　Nearly there ☐　　Nailed it! ☐　　**Spanish exploration**

Spain, c1490

In the 1490s, Spain had ambitions to expand its religious influence and trade prospects abroad. Crusades were used in an attempt to achieve both these aims.

Spain in the 1490s

- Spain had been politically united since 1479 following the marriage of Queen Isabella of Castile and King Ferdinand of Aragon.
- Spain was also religiously united: in the 1490s all Muslims and Jews were expelled if they did not agree to convert to Christianity.
- Spain was emerging as one of the most powerful countries in Europe, rivalled by France to the north and Portugal to the west.

Ferdinand and Isabella, the 'Catholic Monarchs'. Queen Isabella in particular was personally **pious** (deeply religious).

The importance of religion

- Christianity was the main religion in Europe.
- The Catholic Church, led by the pope, was very powerful, in political as well as religious matters.
- The Church had a great influence over people's everyday lives and regular church attendance was expected.
- If the Church, in general, and the pope, in particular, supported a monarch, this would strengthen their power and influence, so it was advantageous to Ferdinand and Isabella to be seen as pious.

The crusading spirit

- The Church at this time wanted to defend the Christian religion from the influence of other religions and to spread Christianity as far as possible.
- The Church supported crusades, which were expeditions to foreign countries, undertaken with the aim of converting the people there to Christianity.
- Initiating and funding crusades meant that Ferdinand and Isabella had the support of the Church and of their people.

Ferdinand and Isabella conquered **Granada** – a Muslim state in southern Spain – in 1492.

Foreign ambitions

- As well as being justified by the aim of converting the local people to Christianity, the exploration and conquest of foreign lands were desirable to expand Spanish influence and provide new trading opportunities.
- Many believed that exploration would open up a new trade route to the East Indies.
- The expeditions would also ensure that Spain, and not Portugal, became the dominant power in southern Europe as it would gain more territory and expand its empire.
- Ferdinand and Isabella also wished to gain new territories for treasure, especially gold and silver.

Piety is the quality of being pious – deeply religious.

Now try this

Write a paragraph explaining why Isabella's personal **piety** was key to her desire to support voyages of exploration and discovery in the 1490s.

Spanish exploration Had a look ☐   Nearly there ☐   Nailed it! ☐

Columbus and sponsorship

In the 1480s, Christopher Columbus, an Italian explorer, looked for sponsorship for his proposed voyage to open up a new sea route to the East Indies.

The race to find a sea route

- Opening up the route to the East Indies would allow many new trading opportunities and potentially large profits.
- Anyone who could establish a trade route by sea, and control over the discovered territories, would gain a huge fortune.
- Interest was strengthened by recent discoveries, in particular that of the Canaries by Spain, and Madeira by Portugal. This made explorers like Columbus believe that there were other new islands and lands that offered enormous opportunities to make money.

The need for financial support

- Voyages of exploration were not cheap as the explorers required ships, provisions and crews who were prepared to risk their lives journeying into the unknown.
- This required financial sponsorship. Sponsors or investors would put up money (capital) in return for a share of the profits made from the voyage.
- Before approaching Isabella and Ferdinand, Columbus had appealed to a number of other European monarchs for support, including the kings of France and Portugal and Henry VII of England, without success.

Why Ferdinand and Isabella granted support in 1491

- ✓ Isabella's personal priest Juan Perez was a friend of Columbus and helped him to present his case to Isabella.
- ✓ A successful expedition would raise Spain's international prestige. Isabella and Ferdinand wanted to establish the trade route and gain control of the territories before their rival, Portugal.
- ✓ The plan had the potential to provide huge income for the Spanish treasury, making the government rich.
- ✓ Isabella, in particular, saw the voyage as an opportunity to spread Christianity to distant lands. This was an important reason for her support for Columbus.

Official support for the 1492 expedition

- Columbus would be entitled to 10 per cent of the produce of any territories discovered.
- If the expedition was successful, he would also receive honours and titles.
- He would be given the title of Grand Admiral of the Ocean Sea.
- He would be appointed governor of any newly colonised lands.

Columbus was able to hire three ships; the *Nina*, the *Pinta* and the *Santa Maria*, as well as the crews he needed to complete his voyage of exploration.

Now try this

Give **one** reason why Ferdinand and Isabella supported Columbus's 1492 voyage of exploration.

Had a look ☐   Nearly there ☐   Nailed it! ☐   Spanish exploration

Columbus's first voyage, 1492

Columbus's voyage of exploration and discovery reached the 'New World' in 1492.

Suitable provisions were needed for a long voyage, including enough preserved food, wine and water to feed the crews for a year, plus items to trade with natives.

Finding ships and crew: the Pinzón brothers helped Columbus to find and equip three ships: the *Nina*, the *Pinta* and the *Santa Maria*.

Martin Pinzón disagreed with Columbus's navigation plans and wanted to turn south as he believed it would take them to Japan. Columbus persuaded him to sail westwards.

Challenges of the voyage

There was a possibility that Portuguese rivals would seek to obstruct Columbus's Atlantic crossing. Columbus adjusted his route to avoid this.

The crew was uneasy about sailing for a long time without sighting land. Columbus kept two logs – one an accurate set and another understating the distance they had travelled, which he showed to the crew.

The voyage and discovery of land

- The expedition left Spain on 3 August, with Columbus captaining the largest ship, the *Santa Maria*.
- On 11 October, land-based birds were spotted. Land was sighted that night.
- On 12 October, Columbus and the Pinzón brothers, with hand-picked members of the crew, rowed ashore and claimed the newly discovered land for Spain.

- Columbus had discovered an island he called San Salvador. Later, he found out that the natives called it Guanahani.
- Almost as soon as they had landed, Columbus and his men were met by a crowd of native people and they traded goods. Columbus remained convinced that he had reached the East Indies.

Columbus's voyage of 1492

The significance of Columbus's voyage

- Columbus had discovered that there was land to the west of Spain and across the Atlantic, although many, including Columbus, believed that they had discovered another sea route to the East Indies.
- This meant that Spain could now claim control of any lands that were discovered by Columbus, or by any other explorer backed by Ferdinand and Isabella.
- However, Spain's claim could be challenged by Portugal, who would also want to send explorers westwards across the Atlantic.

Now try this

Describe **two** challenges Columbus encountered with his voyage of 1492 and how he overcame them.

3

Columbus and the Caribbean — Had a look ☐   Nearly there ☐   Nailed it! ☐

The Bahamas and the Caribbean

Columbus explored the area looking for gold and founded a settlement at La Navidad, Haiti.

Columbus's first contact with the native people

- When Columbus landed on San Salvador he claimed it for Spain.
- In his journal, Columbus described the natives as naked and wearing gold ornaments through holes in their noses.
- Believing he was in the East Indies, Columbus referred to the native people as 'Indians'.
- The people told him that their chief had gold but would not allow Columbus to meet him, saying only that there was gold further south.

Columbus looks for gold

- With the hope of finding gold, Columbus sailed south from San Salvador.
- Having explored several islands (the modern-day Bahamas), Columbus failed to find gold.
- He then landed on a large island the natives had called Colba (modern-day Cuba), believing it was Japan.
- Columbus called the island Isla Juana after Prince Juan, the son of Ferdinand and Isabella.

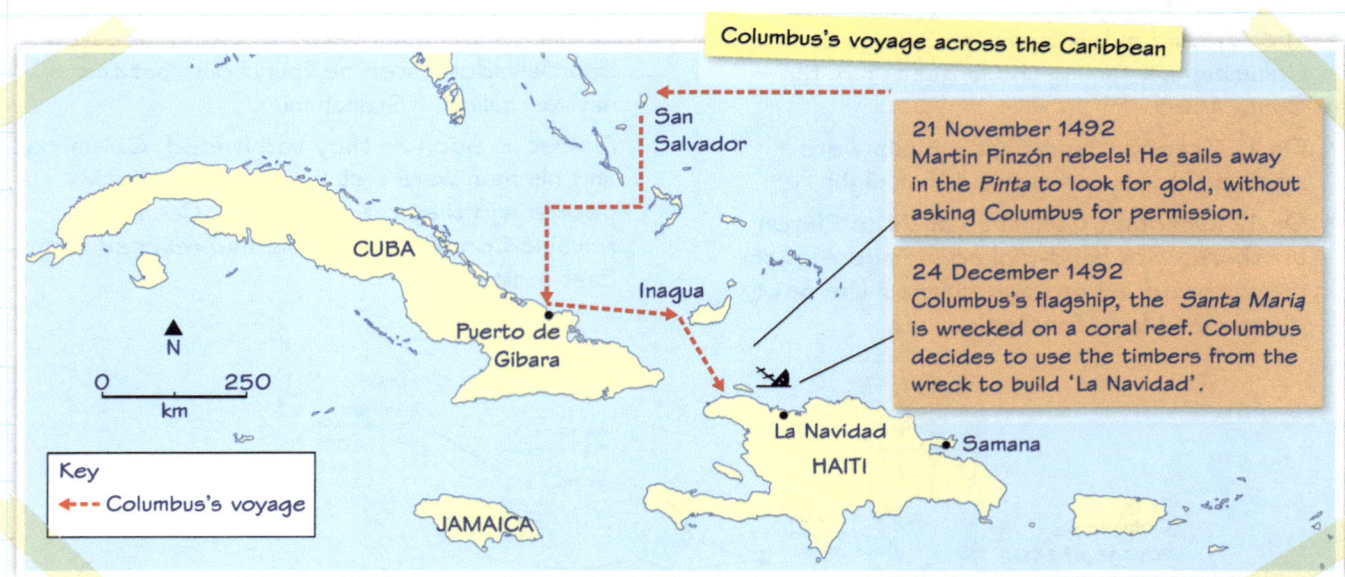

Columbus's voyage across the Caribbean

21 November 1492 Martin Pinzón rebels! He sails away in the *Pinta* to look for gold, without asking Columbus for permission.

24 December 1492 Columbus's flagship, the *Santa Maria* is wrecked on a coral reef. Columbus decides to use the timbers from the wreck to build 'La Navidad'.

The building of La Navidad

- On 21 November 1492, the captain of the *Pinta*, Martin Pinzón, sailed away to look for gold without Columbus's permission.
- Columbus's ship, the *Santa Maria*, ran aground on Christmas Eve, leaving him with only the *Nina* for all his men.
- Columbus built a fort, known as La Navidad, for protection, as there had already been trouble at Samana.

See page 5 for more on this incident.

Columbus returns to Spain

- After the loss of the *Santa Maria*, 39 men had to be left behind at La Navidad to wait for the next Spanish expedition.
- Columbus sailed back to Europe on board the *Nina*, making landfall first in Portugal and then in Spain on 15 March 1493.
- The *Pinta*, having found gold on its solo exploration, rejoined the *Nina*, lost contact again, then landed in northern Spain before returning to port in Palos, in the south.

Now try this

Give **two** reasons why Columbus built the fort known as La Navidad.

Had a look ☐   Nearly there ☐   Nailed it! ☐

Columbus and the Caribbean

Impact of contact with natives

Contact with Caribbean natives in 1492 was peaceful at first, but conflict later arose.

Initial contact and cooperation

- Initial contact was friendly and resulted in trade. In his journal Columbus noted that the natives were more curious than aggressive.
- The Tainos, a tribe of people on Cuba, believed that the Spaniards were 'men from the sky' who would help fulfil their elders' prophecies, so cooperated with them.
- Typically, trade was in hats, balls and glass beads from Spain and cotton, parrots and javelins from the islands.
- The native people helped the Spanish unload the *Santa Maria* when it struck a reef off the coast of Haiti.

Gold, cotton and tobacco, 1492–93

- Columbus found small amounts of gold on Haiti but Martin Pinzón soon found more on a nearby island.
- Cotton was seen growing on Cuba, San Salvador and on other islands in the Bahamas.
- The 'cotton' the Spanish saw was actually kapok, which could be spun and woven like cotton.
- Tobacco was given to Columbus as a gift by a native chief in San Salvador.
- The Spanish quickly adopted the native practice of smoking tobacco rolled into cigars.

Relations with the native people

- In his journal Columbus noted that the Tainos were peaceful, would make good slaves and would be easily converted to Christianity.
- In contrast, Columbus described the Caribs as 'ferocious', engaged in cannibalism and in raiding other tribes looking for slaves and women. He also wrote about the shrunken heads seen in a Carib village.

Artist's drawing of a Carib village

The first conflict at Samana

The success of the Spanish expedition depended on finding large quantities of gold, which brought them into conflict with some tribes.

↓

The first incident happened at Samana, Haiti, where the *Nina* was forced to anchor during a storm.

↓

Going ashore to look for gold, the Spanish were attacked by the natives. In the violence that followed, two of the native people were wounded and the rest escaped.

↓

The incident showed that the native people were prepared to attack, so the Spanish would need to be ready to defend themselves.

↓

Columbus was already prepared to use force to achieve the expedition's objective of finding gold, but after the incident at Samana he wrote in his journal that the natives must be made to fear the Spanish.

Now try this

Write a short paragraph about why the incident at Samana was important.

Columbus and the Caribbean

Had a look ☐ Nearly there ☐ Nailed it! ☐

Rivalry with Portugal

Portugal and Spain both believed they had a claim to the New World – the dispute was resolved through the Treaty of Tordesillas, 1494.

Columbus's return to Spain

> Columbus recrossed the Atlantic, arriving first at Lisbon in Portugal on 4 March 1493.
>
> ⬇
>
> Soon after his arrival in Palos, Spain, on 15 March 1493, Columbus was warmly congratulated by Ferdinand and Isabella and allowed to accompany them to Barcelona in triumph.
>
> ⬇
>
> He received the titles promised to him when Ferdinand and Isabella had originally agreed to sponsor the expedition.

See page 2 for a list of the titles and financial rewards promised to Columbus.

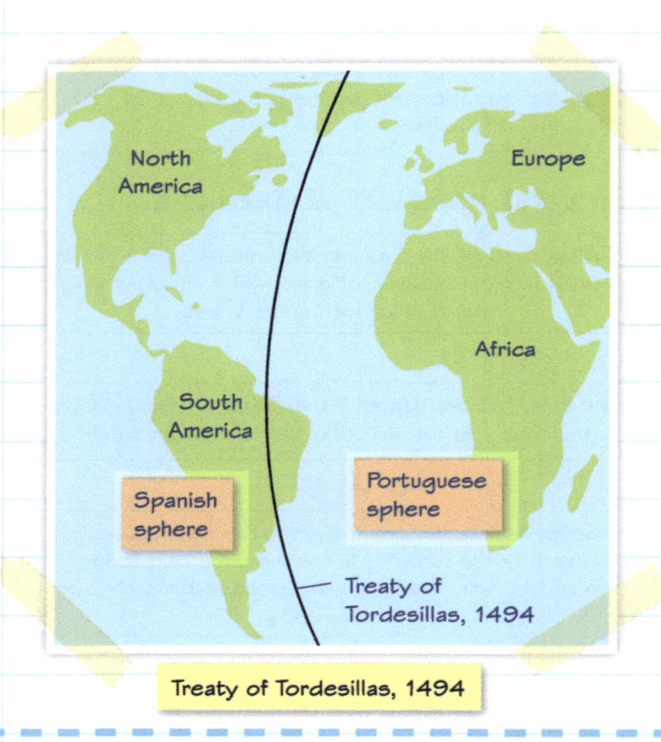

The Portuguese claim the New World

- King John of Portugal soon heard about Columbus's expedition and the existence of a New World across the Atlantic.
- Portugal now claimed that it, not Spain, had the right to rule the New World, based on an agreement, the Treaty of Alcacovas of 1479, which stated that all lands to the west belonged to Portugal.
- Ferdinand and Isabella rejected John's claim to any part of the New World and assembled a fleet of ships in southern Spain close to Portugal: war seemed likely.

The Treaty of Tordesillas, 1494

- The intervention of Pope Alexander VI resolved the dispute.
- The pope supported Spain's claim because of Isabella's piety: he believed that Spain would spread Christianity in the New World.

See page 1 for more on the importance of religion.

- Under the Treaty, a line was drawn from the North Pole to the South Pole, 2000 km to the west of Cape Verde. All lands to the west of this line were Spanish. All lands to the east, with the exception of the Canaries, were Portuguese.
- The New World was all Spanish, except for some easterly parts of South America. The exploration and control of Africa was left to the Portuguese.

Treaty of Tordesillas, 1494

Why was the Treaty of Tordesillas important?

- The treaty gave Spain most of the New World. Ferdinand and Isabella were now in a position to claim Mexico, North America and most of South America, in addition to the Caribbean.
- This meant that any gold and silver found in these territories would go only to Spain.
- Spain now had a major incentive to explore further and conquer much of the New World: as a way of obtaining gold, silver, tobacco and other resources.

Now try this

In **one** paragraph, explain the terms of the Treaty of Tordesillas of 1494.

Had a look ☐   Nearly there ☐   Nailed it! ☐   Spanish claims

Columbus's other voyages

Columbus made three further voyages: two as Spanish governor of the Caribbean settlements between 1493 and 1500, and a final voyage from 1502 to 1504.

1 Columbus's second voyage, 1493–96
- As 'Viceroy of the Indies', Columbus was in charge of the new territories.
- He was given a fleet of 17 ships carrying about 1200 people: priests, gentlemen, farmers and skilled craft workers as well as animals, seeds and tools.

Turn to page 3 to read about the first voyage of 1492.

2 Columbus as governor
- Columbus was responsible for establishing a colony of settlements in the discovered lands in the Caribbean.
- His aims were to treat the natives well and convert them to Christianity, and to send back gold to the Spanish government.
- He had the power to appoint officials to act on his behalf.

4 Columbus returns to Spain
- Leaving his brother Bartholomew in charge at Isabela, in 1494 Columbus left to explore the southern coastline of Cuba.
- Straight away, Bartholomew started building a new settlement at Santo Domingo.
- Columbus reached Spain in June 1496 to report on progress and respond to criticisms of his governance of Isabela.

3 The foundation of Isabela, 1493
- Columbus founded a new settlement 'Isabela', but it was unsuccessful because of the poor location and because most Spanish settlers were more interested in finding gold and troubling the local women than in clearing the forest for planting crops.
- With no experience of running a settlement, Columbus was unable to control the Spanish settlers and became angry because of the conflict they caused.

5 The significance of Santo Domingo
- Columbus returned from Spain in 1498 to find the settlement at Santo Domingo in an uproar.
- He was able to calm matters for a while by offering the settlers special rights, including land and native labourers to work on it.
- The rebellion continued and Columbus responded by hanging some Spaniards and natives; unable to control the colony, he requested help from Ferdinand and Isabella.
- The Spanish government sent its own representative, Francisco de Bobadilla, to replace Columbus as governor in 1500. He upheld the settlers' grievances and Columbus was returned to Spain in chains to face trial.

6 Columbus's trial and final voyage
- Columbus and Bartholomew were accused of tyranny, brutality and incompetence and imprisoned for six weeks.
- Ferdinand and Isabella allowed Columbus to keep his titles but ordered he should no longer have any say in the government of the territories in the Caribbean.
- Columbus undertook a fourth voyage between May 1502 and November 1504 but by this time Isabella had died and Ferdinand refused to meet him on his return.

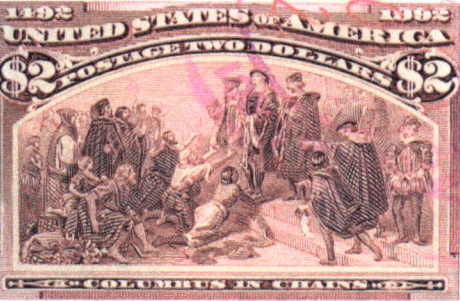

'Columbus In Chains' was part of a series of postage stamps issued in the USA in 1892 to celebrate the 400th anniversary of Columbus's discovery of the New World.

Now try this

1. Describe the key events that led to Columbus's return to Spain in disgrace in 1500.
2. In a short summary, explain the significance of the revolt at Santo Domingo.

Spanish claims | Had a look ☐　Nearly there ☐　Nailed it! ☐

Effects of Spanish settlement

Spanish settlement, from 1493 onwards, had significant effects on the New World and especially on the native population.

The development of a Spanish Empire in the New World

The discovery of inhabited lands on the other side of the Atlantic Ocean presented Ferdinand and Isabella with opportunities:

- They could encourage Spanish settlers to colonise the land and develop their crusading spirit by converting previously unknown lands to Christianity.
- They could also use any gold and silver found in the New World to boost the wealth of the Spanish government and increase Spain's power and influence in the world.

However, any Spanish Empire in the New World had to find a way of governing the native population.

> The **New World** referred to lands colonised in the western hemisphere including the Caribbean, the Bermudas and the American mainland.

The development of slavery:
- Under Columbus, the Spanish organised expeditions to capture slaves and send them to the slave markets of Spain. This policy was stopped by Isabella, who freed and returned many of the natives.
- However, under Governor Ovando the *encomienda* system was established, whereby each Spanish settler was allocated a group of natives who had to provide tribute in the form of labour, goods, or both. In return, the Spanish would 'protect' the natives, teach them Spanish and convert them to Christianity. In practice, this meant that many natives were exploited like slaves.

Gold and tribute:
- Natives were required to pay tribute to the Spanish in the form of gold, cotton or produce.
- The development of gold mining under Bobadilla and his successor, Ovando, meant that natives were instead required to work under harsh conditions in the gold mines set up by the Spanish as virtual slaves.

The effects of Spanish settlement in the New World

Disease and death:
- The Spanish brought with them new diseases, including smallpox and measles. The native people had no immunity to these infections and many died.
- This had a devastating effect on the native population. In Hispaniola (Haiti) there were an estimated 500 000 natives in 1492. By 1507 this had fallen to 60 000.

Native rebellions and Spanish repression:
- Natives who resisted slavery were treated brutally – many were mutilated or attacked by hunting dogs. During Columbus's governorship, and afterwards, some natives revolted.
- The Spanish responded brutally to revolt. In the Jaragua massacre (1503) the Spanish killed Tainos, burning them alive in the meeting house where they had gathered. Similarly, in the Higuey massacre hundreds of Tainos – men, women and children – were slaughtered by the Spanish.

Now try this

Describe **two** ways in which natives were affected by Spanish settlement in the New World.

Had a look ☐ Nearly there ☐ Nailed it! ☐

Spanish claims

Development of an imperial policy

Following Columbus's discovery of the New World, the Spanish government needed to develop an imperial policy to enable it to control trade and religion in the newly discovered lands.

Regulation of exploration:
- In 1495, Ferdinand and Isabella issued a decree (lawful *command*) controlling exploration in the New World.
- It stated that any ship going to the New World had to be registered in, and leave from, Cadiz.
- One-tenth of the cargo on ships going to the New World had to be Spanish.
- People were free to live or prospect for gold in the New World but had to give two-thirds of the gold found and one-tenth of all other products to the Spanish treasury.
- The discovery of any new lands had to be registered with the Spanish authorities.

Establishment of a monopoly on trade:
- In 1503, a government agency was established in Seville.
- The aim of the *Casa de Contratacion* (House of Trade) was to ensure that Spain controlled all trade with the Caribbean, and that a proportion of the trade profits were paid to the Spanish treasury.
- Traders had to have permission from this agency before they could trade, giving Spain complete control over trade with the New World.

Spanish imperial policy in the New World

Extension of Spanish authority:
- After a hurricane in 1502 wrecked the town, Santo Domingo was rebuilt and developed as the control centre of Spanish government in the New World.
- From here the governor ruled the new Spanish territories on behalf of the Spanish government.

Use of missionaries to convert the native population:
- Catholic monks and priests accompanied the Spanish settlers in Haiti and elsewhere.
- Their role was to teach natives about Christianity and baptise them as Christians.
- They also taught reading and writing and discouraged the natives from following 'pagan' customs.

The Laws of Burgos, 1512:
- The Laws of Burgos were ordered by Ferdinand and applied to the whole of the New World.
- These laws maintained the *encomienda* system, which, in practice, turned the natives into slaves.

To read about the *encomienda* system, see page 8.

- The laws allowed Spanish officials to punish natives who broke the laws.
- They required natives to be instructed in Christianity.
- They set down that Indians were to be treated kindly and their hours of work regulated.

Natives working for the Spanish settlers

Spanish imperial policy ended the traditional way of life for natives, requiring them to convert to Christianity, live in towns and work, often as slaves, for the Spanish.

Now try this

In **one** paragraph, explain the significance of the Laws of Burgos, 1512.

Think about how the laws shaped the relationship between the Spanish and the native people.

Start of an empire   Had a look ☐   Nearly there ☐   Nailed it! ☐

Balboa and the conquistadors, 1513–28

Between 1513 and about 1528, the Spanish conquistadors conquered Panama, Cuba, Mexico and Peru, and circumnavigated the globe.

Who were the conquistadors?

- The conquistadors (a Spanish/Portuguese word meaning 'conqueror') were professional soldiers who took part in expeditions to explore and conquer lands in Central and South America.
- Officially only Spanish Catholics could act as conquistadors, but many were actually foreign mercenaries hoping to become rich by acting on behalf of the Spanish government.

The conquistadors were accompanied by Catholic priests whose aim was to convert natives to Christianity.

Balboa, conquistador

- ✓ Balboa was a conquistador whose major motive was to gain wealth.
- ✓ He arrived in Central America as early as 1509 and by 1511 had become governor of Veragua.
- ✓ In 1513, he led an expedition that discovered the Pacific Ocean.
- ✓ He was ruthless: the native people were treated brutally.
- ✓ The possibility of great wealth, in the form of gold, silver and pearls, led to rivalry between Balboa and Pedrarias (another ambitious conquistador).
- ✓ In 1519, Balboa was executed for treason in Acla by Pedrarias, who replaced him as governor.

The discovery of the Pacific, 1513

- In 1513, Balboa led an expedition that crossed the isthmus of Panama and discovered the Pacific.
- Balboa claimed the sea and the land that surrounded it for Spain.
- The new route meant that Spain was free to conquer lands on the Pacific coast.

The founding and significance of Panama

- Panama was founded as a Spanish territory under Pedrarias as royal governor, and became important as a colony.
- From there, Pedrarias and his second-in-command, Espinosa, explored the Pacific coast.
- The route through Panama led to Magellan's circumnavigation of the globe.

See page 12 to revise Magellan.

- Panama became a starting point for further conquests by Cortes and by Pizarro.

Turn to pages 13–15 for more about Cortes, and pages 17–19 for more about Pizarro.

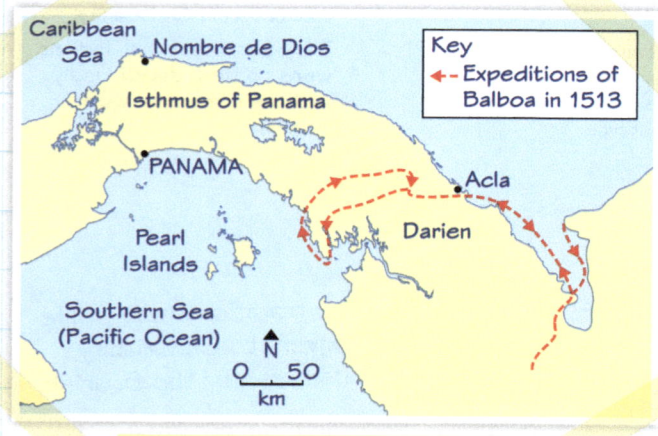

The expeditions of Balboa, 1513

Now try this

Give **two** reasons why Balboa's expeditions in Central America were so important.

Had a look ☐   Nearly there ☐   Nailed it! ☐

Start of an empire

The conquest of Cuba

Between 1511 and 1514, Diego Velázquez conquered Cuba, giving Spain complete control over the Caribbean.

Key events in the conquest of Cuba

Timeline

1511 To obtain more slaves and plunder the gold and silver of Cuba, Velázquez launched an invasion. He also wanted to capture Hatuey, a native chief who had escaped from Haiti with 300 followers.

1513 At Caonao, 2000 native people were massacred by the Spanish, who ran amok in the village.

1514 Cuba was established as a Spanish colony under Velázquez. Spanish settlements were constructed at Santiago de Cuba and Havana.

By 1511 Death from illness had greatly reduced the number of people available to work as slaves in Haiti and in other islands controlled by the Spanish.

1512 Despite strong native resistance, Hatuey was captured. Having refused to convert to Christianity he was burned to death.

By 1514 The rest of the island was conquered by the Spanish.

The burning of the native chief Hatuey in 1512. He had tried to warn tribes in Cuba of the dangers posed by the Spanish.

The significance of the capture of Cuba

- The *encomienda* system was established in Cuba with the Spanish as masters and the natives as virtual slaves.

Look back at page 8 for more on the *encomienda* system.

- This allowed for the cultivation of crops, especially tobacco, on the island.
- The native population declined further – from about 350,000 in 1514 to about 3000 by 1555 – and from the mid-1500s African slaves were brought to Cuba.
- Spanish control of Cuba led to further exploration and conquest on the mainland, including of Florida and Mexico.

Cruelty to native people

- The natives were treated appallingly by the Spanish. Many were forced to work in gold mines and on cotton plantations.
- This prevented many of them from planting the crops that they had farmed for centuries. Many starved as a result.
- Others were murdered or enslaved.
- Native people were required to convert to Christianity. Those who refused to do so were burned as pagans and heretics.

A **heretic** is a non-believer: someone who believes something that is against the accepted religion, or acts against it.

Now try this

In a few short paragraphs, summarise in your own words the Spanish conquest of Cuba between 1511 and 1514.

11

Start of an empire · Had a look ☐ · Nearly there ☐ · Nailed it! ☐

The voyage of Magellan

Magellan's voyage around the globe resulted in the opening up of the Pacific for trade and exploration and gave Spain control over the Philippines.

The quest for the Spice Islands

- In 1518, the newly crowned Charles I of Spain placed Ferdinand Magellan in command of five ships to sail across the Atlantic and find a new route to the **Spice Islands** (part of the East Indies) and new lands for Spain.

> The Spice Islands were famous for their large amounts of mace, nutmeg and pepper.

- The Treaty of Tordesillas did not specify whether the Spice Islands belonged to Spain or Portugal.
- Charles wanted Magellan to find the islands first for Spain, to develop trade in spices.
- Magellan was keen to take up the challenge to find the new sea route.

Magellan's journey

- In 1519, Magellan set sail westwards and southwards across the Atlantic, entering the Pacific by discovering the narrow strait at the tip of South America, later named after him.
- He sailed to the Philippines, which he reached in 1521, claiming them for Spain.

> Magellan was later killed in the Philippines by natives.

- In 1522, having sailed westwards across the Indian Ocean, only one of the five ships, the *Victoria*, returned to port in Spain. Of the 270 men who had set out in 1519 only 18 returned, many of them very sick.

Why was Magellan's voyage important?

- It established that the earth was round and that Columbus was correct in his belief that the East Indies could be reached by sailing westwards.
- It opened up the Pacific, leading to the exploration of the East Indies and the Philippines. Ships could also sail up the Pacific coast opening up the west coast of North America to exploration and trade. By the mid-1540s, places such as California were being visited by Spanish explorers.
- It meant that the Philippines became part of the Spanish Empire. This, together with the Spanish Empire in the New World, enabled Spain to dominate world trade by the 1540s, with tobacco, spices, silver and gold all being traded by Spanish ships. This also meant that the income of the Spanish government increased as gold, silver and taxes rolled into its treasury.

Magellan's voyage around the world

- 20 September 1519 Start of voyage.
- 27 April 1521 Magellan and others killed by natives. No one to crew *Concepcion* so ship burned.
- 8 September 1522 *Victoria* reaches Seville.
- March–April 1520 Crews of *Victoria*, *Concepcion* and *San Antonio* mutiny. *Santiago* sent ahead and is wrecked.
- 16 March 1521 Lands on island of Hononham.
- 13–27 December 1519 Fresh supplies at Rio de Janiero.
- 21 December 1521 *Victoria* sets off for Spain. *Trinidad* left behind for repair.
- 22 May 1522
- 21 October–1 November 1520 Magellan decides on this route to the Pacific. Captain and crew of *San Antonio* disagree and return to Spain. *Victoria*, *Concepcion* and *Trinidad* enter what is now the Strait of Magellan, reaching the Pacific on 28 November.

Key: ← Magellan's route

Now try this

Explain why Charles I was keen for Magellan to find the Spice Islands.

Had a look ☐   Nearly there ☐   Nailed it! ☐   **Conquest of Mexico**

Expedition to Mexico, 1519

Cortes's 1519 expedition to Mexico resulted in the collapse of the Aztec Empire and in Spanish control over Central America.

Why did the Spanish send an expedition to Mexico?

- Explorers who had returned the year before brought back beautiful gold and silver objects and stories of stone cities built by the Mayans.
- Velázquez, the ambitious governor of Cuba, wanted the wealth and fame that would result from claiming more land for Spain, as well as Church approval for spreading Christianity.
- Working for Velázquez in Cuba, Cortes had become wealthy. The prospect of more treasure made Cortes willing to launch an expedition to Mexico.

Rivalry between Velázquez and Cortes

> Velázquez appointed Cortes as the commander of the expedition to Mexico.

> Cortes was responsible for establishing trading relations with the tribes living along the coast, but ordered not to settle on the mainland.

> Realising that Cortes might ignore his orders and conquer the territory, Velázquez changed his mind about having Cortes in charge just before the expedition was due to sail.

> Velázquez set out to arrest Cortes and stop him from setting sail but was too late. Cortes had been warned and had already left Cuba with 11 ships and about 600 men and 100 Cuban slaves.

Mexico in 1519

- Mexico was dominated by the Aztec Empire, which had existed for hundreds of years and was ruled by Montezuma.
- Rulers of the conquered cities could remain in power provided they paid tribute and supplied the Aztecs with warriors as necessary.
- Many tribes resented Aztec rule and were potential allies for Cortes and the Spanish against the Aztecs.
- The Aztec capital Tenochtitlan, a city of about 300,000 people in the centre of Lake Texcoco, was larger than any European city.

Cortes's arrival in Mexico

- In March 1519, Cortes landed in Mexico, formally claiming it for Spain.
- He then proceeded to the Tabasco River where he won a battle against the native tribes – the Mayans. Cortes owed much of his success to horses and artillery, which the Mayans did not have, giving him a significant military advantage.
- He was given 20 young native women, converting them to Christianity. Among these women was Malinche, who became both his mistress and interpreter. She spoke with both the Aztecs and other tribes on Cortes's behalf. Cortes was now in a position to meet and negotiate with the Aztecs.

Now try this

In your own words, give **two** reasons why the Spanish were prepared to launch an expedition to Mexico in 1519.

Conquest of Mexico

Had a look ☐ Nearly there ☐ Nailed it! ☐

Key events of the conquest

By building alliances with the local tribe, the Tlaxcalans, Cortes was able to overthrow Montezuma and defeat the Aztec Empire.

Montezuma's invitation to Cortes

✓ Montezuma's Aztec spies had been tracking Cortes. They were concerned about the alliances and agreements made by Cortes with native tribes who disliked the Aztecs.

✓ Montezuma sent gifts to Cortes, inviting him and his soldiers to come to Tenochtitlan, the capital of the Aztec Empire, as his guests.

✓ The Aztecs suggested that the Spaniards travelled to Tenochtitlan through the sacred city of Cholula, which was under Aztec control. This may have reflected Montezuma's belief that the Spanish were gods who came from the sea.

✓ Cortes, fearing a trap, agreed that he would travel to Tenochtitlan via Cholula but also accepted the Tlaxcalan offer to provide 1000 warriors to go with him.

The massacre at Cholula

- On the way to Tenochtitlan, Cortes's soldiers entered Cholula and massacred 3000 people and destroyed the city, which was sacred to the Aztecs.
- This sent shock waves around the Aztec Empire and demonstrated the power of the Spanish.
- The Spanish and their Tlaxcalan allies now began to advance on Tenochtitlan.

The massacre at Cholula

The Spanish arrival in Tenochtitlan, 1519

Montezuma initially welcomed the Spanish as guests, perhaps believing that they were gods.

However, Cortes tricked Montezuma, taking him prisoner and threatening to kill anyone who opposed the Spanish.

Cortes forced Montezuma to act as a puppet king, ruling the Aztec Empire according to Cortes's instructions.

Christian images were put on Aztec temples to show that the Christian God was superior to Aztec gods.

The defeat of the Aztecs, 1520–21

- In April 1520, 1000 Spanish sent by Velázquez to arrest Cortes landed in Mexico.
- Leaving his deputy Alvarado in charge at Tenochtitlan, Cortes defeated Velázquez's forces, many of whom defected to Cortes.
- Alvarado, fearing a rebellion, killed the Aztec nobles who had defied him.
- This led to the Night of Tears (June 1520): the Aztecs turned on the Spanish, killing half and driving the rest of them and their Tlaxcalan allies out.
- Montezuma was killed, either by the Spanish as they fled the city or by his own people.
- Cortes and his allies regrouped and besieged Tenochtitlan, starving the inhabitants before attacking. On 13 August 1521, the city surrendered to the Spanish.

Now try this

Give **one** reason why the Spanish succeeded in capturing Tenochtitlan between November 1519 and August 1521.

Had a look ☐   Nearly there ☐   Nailed it! ☐   Spain's impact

Cortes's actions, 1523–28

The capture of Tenochtitlan marked the end of the Aztec Empire, enabling Cortes, as governor and captain-general, to turn Central America into New Spain.

Cortes's actions as governor and captain-general

Cortes, first governor of New Spain

- Cortes built Mexico City on the site of Tenochtitlan, destroying all Aztec religious temples.

- In 1523, Cortes was named governor and captain-general of New Spain. Four royal officials were appointed to help him govern and keep an eye on him. They reported to the Council of the Indies and, through it, to the King.

- Within a short time, Cortes had many of the Aztecs' political and religious leaders killed, leaving the people unable to challenge the Spanish.

- He allocated land to the Spaniards, encouraged others to settle there and set up the encomienda system.

- He developed industry, including the manufacture of textiles, sugar cane and iron products.

- Cortes took tributes from other tribal leaders, including the Tlaxcalans. This was normally paid in gold or maize.

- He developed Mexican agriculture by importing sheep, goats, vines and silk worms from Cuba and Spain. One of his aims was to make Mexico self-sufficient in food.

- Under Cortes, thousands of natives were converted to Christianity. From 1523 onwards hundreds of Franciscan friars went out to New Spain, where they founded the Church in Mexico.

See pages 8–11 for a reminder of what the encomienda system was.

Cortes: misrule and demotion, 1528

- Cortes was unpopular with some conquistadors – he was accused of **misrule** (governing badly), including stealing gold that he had found when the Spanish captured Tenochtitlan.
- Cortes returned to Spain to explain himself in 1528 and tried to impress Charles I with his conquests and the treasure he had collected for Spain.
- Charles **demoted** him to captain-general but allowed him to keep his land. However, the position of governor was given to a rival.

When someone is **demoted** or receives a **demotion**, they are moved to a lower status. This is often done as a punishment.

The extension of Spanish rule

- Spanish explorers were encouraged to launch expeditions to expand Spanish influence in Central America.

The explorers were motivated by the search for gold, and the story of El Dorado – a city paved with gold.

- Expeditions were sent to Zacatula on the Pacific coast and to Oaxaca, the main gold-producing region of Mexico.
- Cortes developed new cities, including Mexico City. He also developed mining, including iron and silver. Many natives were employed there, often as slaves.

The conquest of the huge Aztec Empire led Charles I to establish the Council of the Indies in 1524.

Now try this

Explain **two** ways in which Cortes tried to strengthen Spanish rule in Mexico.

Think about how Cortes's actions made the Aztecs weak and the Spanish strong.

Spain's impact — Had a look ☐   Nearly there ☐   Nailed it! ☐

Consequences for the Aztecs

The Spanish invasion had far-reaching effects for the Aztecs.

How were the Aztecs affected by the Spanish conquest of Mexico?

The destruction of the Aztec ruling class: The position of the emperor was abolished while the Aztec nobility and priests were executed, depriving the people of Aztec leadership.

The end of the Aztec Empire: The lands now became New Spain and part of a growing Spanish Empire. The governor was responsible for governing the territory on behalf of the Spanish king.

Intermarriage between the Spanish and the Aztecs: By 1550, three groups were established; the Spanish settlers, the Mestizo (people who were half Spanish/half native) and the Aztecs.

Religious conflict: The Aztec religion was abolished as blasphemy. Aztec priests were murdered and temples pulled down.

Colonisation: Spanish settlers were encouraged to come from Spain and Cuba and given land under the *encomienda* system. Less land was left for the Aztecs which meant that many could not provide for their families and had to work for the Spanish.

The destruction of Aztec religious images

Language change: Spanish now became the main language in New Spain although native languages were still spoken.

See page 8 to revise how the encomienda system worked.

Forced conversion to Christianity: Many Aztecs did not want to convert, and worshipped the Christian God in public but their old gods in private.

Agricultural change: The Spanish introduced meat and dairy farming as well as wheat and other cereals, changing the diet of the natives.

Disease: The Aztecs were exposed to diseases, such as smallpox and measles. The population of Mexico in 1519 was about 25 million; by 1555 it was about 6.2 million. Disease was a significant factor in this fall in population.

Industrial change: The Spanish now mined iron, gold and silver, and grew cotton and tobacco commercially, all made possible by Aztec slave labour.

Aztec society accepted many Spanish systems as they were similar to some of their existing social structures.

Notice how some of the consequences for the Aztecs of the Spanish invasion are linked.

*Remember to explain and not describe. To explain you need to say **how** or **why** the Aztecs were affected by the Spanish conquest.*

Now try this

Explain **two** ways in which the Aztecs were affected by the Spanish conquest of Mexico.

Had a look ☐   Nearly there ☐   Nailed it! ☐   Spain's impact

Pizarro and Panama

Francisco Pizarro, a conquistador and mayor of Panama city, launched a series of expeditions southwards to find Peru, which eventually brought him into contact with the Incas.

Pizarro's ambitions

- ✓ Pizarro had been with Balboa in 1513 when the expedition reached the Pacific.
  > You can revise the journeys of Balboa on page 10.
- ✓ Pizarro was impressed by accounts of Cortes's success in Mexico.
- ✓ He had also heard stories from traders who told him of Inca wealth and about 'Pirú' – a great land to the south rich with gold.

Pizarro's first expedition, 1524

- ✓ In November 1524, Pizarro led an expedition southwards with about 80 men and 40 horses.
- ✓ This first expedition was not a success. It sailed down the Pacific coast, reaching only Colombia before bad weather, lack of food and attacks by hostile natives forced Pizarro to turn back.

Pizarro's expeditions in the New World

Pizarro's second expedition, 1526–27

In November 1526, Pizarro left Panama with two ships, 180 men and some horses.

↓

He reached as far as the Colombian San Juan River.

↓

He discovered and captured a raft containing silver, gold, silver and emeralds.

↓

In spite of demands that Pizarro return to Panama, he and 13 other men ('The Famous Thirteen') decided to stay and explore the area further.

↓

They journeyed southwards on an improvised vessel and found evidence of fabulous wealth, including gold and silver in northern Peru.

↓

Pizarro returned to Panama in 1527.

Pizarro's appeal to the Spanish King Charles I

- In 1528, Pizarro returned to Spain with evidence of Inca wealth, including llamas, silver and gold.
- Having been refused permission to launch a third expedition by the governor of Panama, he appealed to Charles I, promising to 'extend the empire of Castile'.
- Pizarro received a licence, the *Capitulacion de Toledo*, in July 1529, authorising him to conquer Peru.

Now try this

In a short paragraph, describe the impact of Pizarro's second expedition to Peru, 1526–27.

17

Conquest of the Incas — Had a look ☐ Nearly there ☐ Nailed it! ☐

Pizarro's arrival in Peru

Pizarro's third expedition arrived in Peru in 1532 to find an empire weakened by smallpox.

The Inca Empire

- Huayna Capac, the powerful Inca emperor, was worshipped as a god by his people.
- The empire stretched down the west coast of Latin America along the Andes mountains.
- It contained huge cities, temples and fortresses, linked by a network of roads.
- The empire was fabulously wealthy and contained gold and silver mines.

The significance of Huayna Capac's death

- In 1528, an outbreak of smallpox killed thousands of Incas, including many of Huayna Capac's advisers and generals, and then Huayna Capac himself.
- Huayna Capac left the empire to his two sons, Atahuallpa and Huascar, who divided the empire between them. Atahuallpa got the northern half and Huascar the southern half. This resulted in a civil war between the two rulers.

> Atahuallpa eventually defeated Huascar's army. He was afraid that Huascar would join the Spanish, and had him murdered.

Pizarro's third expedition, 1530–32

- Pizarro left Panama in December 1530, arriving in Ecuador in January 1531.
- He realised that the civil war between the brothers gave him a chance to seize power by attacking when the empire was divided, and weakened by disease.
- Pizarro arrived in Peru in April 1532 and approached Atahuallpa's camp on 15 November 1532.
- When invited to take a ceremonial drink in gold cups, the Spanish poured the drink away and threatened the Incas by riding their horses near them.
- Atahuallpa invited Pizarro to meet him the next day in the town square at Cajamarca, where they would be given lodgings at the palace.

> Pizarro and Vicente deliberately engineered this situation, provoking Atahuallpa and giving them the excuse to attack the Incas.

Pizarro declared the Inca Empire annexed by Spain. This included coastal areas such as Chile, which the Spanish began to explore in the 1530s.

The Battle of Cajamarca, 16 November 1532

- The Spanish arrived early and hid their men in ambush positions in the square.
- Atahuallpa was offered a Christian Bible by Friar Vicente, but threw it on the ground, arguing that the Christian God was no better than those of the Incas.
- When Vicente argued that the Incas were heretics, the Spanish ambushed them, 'killing them like ants'. Thousands of Incas were killed and Atahuallpa was taken prisoner.

Now try this

Create a timeline of events from Pizarro's departure for Peru in 1530 to the capture of Atahuallpa.

Had a look ☐   Nearly there ☐   Nailed it! ☐   Conquest of the Incas

Pizarro's conquest of Peru

In 1533, Pizarro had Atahuallpa executed and installed Manco, his half-brother, on the throne, leading to the Inca revolt and the siege of Cuzco, 1536–37.

The murder of Atahuallpa, 1533

- The Spanish agreed to ransom Atahuallpa for a room full of gold and double the amount of silver.
- However, the Spanish did not release him. Instead they accused him of plotting against them and put him on trial for treason.
- Atahuallpa was executed in Cajamarca town square as his Inca supporters pleaded for his life.

Pizarro puts Manco on the throne

- Pizarro marched from Cajamarca to Cuzco, the Inca capital, and was welcomed by the inhabitants, many of whom had hated Atahuallpa's rule and the civil war.
- Pizarro had Manco, a younger son of Huayna Capac and half-brother of Atahuallpa, crowned as the new Inca emperor.

For a reminder about the Inca Emperor Huayna Capac, go to page 18.

The revolt of the Incas, 1536

- The Spanish saw Manco as a puppet king who would rule on their behalf.
- This led to an Inca revolt when Manco escaped from the Spanish, assembled an army and attacked the Spanish base at Cuzco.

The Siege of Cuzco

The Siege of Cuzco, 1536–37

10000 Inca warriors faced 150 Spanish and 1000 native allies.

↓

The Inca warriors broke into the town, burning buildings to try to drive out the Spanish, but the Spanish were able to put the fires out.

↓

The Spanish used their cavalry to attack the Inca warriors.

↓

The Spanish captured the fortress of Sacsahuaman from the Incas, which the Inca army then besieged.

↓

The siege ended when Spanish forces exploring Chile returned.

↓

Manco withdrew and established a separate kingdom (the Neo Inca State) which lasted until 1572.

The impact of the conquest

- Pizarro governed Peru until his death at the hands of rival conquistadors in 1541.
- Pizarro and his government were based in Lima, the city they built in Peru. The conquistadors took gold, silver and other commodities from the area, shipping some back to Spain.
- The Inca Empire was settled by Spaniards — not only conquistadors but also Spanish merchants who saw an opportunity to make money.
- The conquest led to the destruction of Inca civilisation. Many Incas were reduced to slavery and were joined by further slaves brought in from Africa.
- Disease, especially smallpox and measles, devastated the Inca population, reducing it by 93 per cent by 1591.

Now try this

Give **two** reasons why the Incas revolted in 1536.

Expansion of empire — Had a look ☐   Nearly there ☐   Nailed it! ☐

Discovery of silver in Bolivia and Mexico

The discovery of silver led to the development of mining towns with the increased use of slave labour, and brought significant wealth to the Spanish Empire.

The discovery of silver in the New World

- One of the conquistadors' principal motives for exploration was the discovery of gold and silver.
- By 1550, silver had been discovered in Potosi (Bolivia) and in Guanajuato and Zacatecas (Mexico).
- Some of it had to be sent back to Spain, but the conquistadors kept much of the wealth.

The Potosi silver mine in Bolivia

Silver mining and processing

- Deep mines were dug where there was no risk of flooding (pumps were not available).
- Silver ore was mined and brought to the surface.
- The ore was then **smelted** to extract the silver, which was turned into silver coins.
- Many workers were needed to bring the silver ore to the surface and to smelt the ore.
- Many pack animals were needed to move the silver.

See page 23 to revise the effect of silver on the Spanish economy.

Smelting is a process that uses high temperatures to extract metal.

The significance of silver in Bolivia and Mexico

The need for vast amounts of labour to extract and smelt the silver ore led to the development of mining towns at Potosi, Guanajuato and Zacatecas. They started as camps made up of tents but developed quickly into towns housing large numbers of people employed in mining.

This led to the circulation of rumours and legends that there was a vast amount of undiscovered wealth in the New World. The most famous example of this was El Dorado, the so-called 'City of Gold' which was rumoured to be somewhere in America.

This encouraged many Spanish merchants to invest in projects designed to explore the area further in the hope of finding more gold and silver, leading to further explorations and expeditions to California, Venezuela and Argentina during the 16th century.

This resulted in increased colonisation of the New World as the conquistadors were joined by adventurers, merchants and speculators, as well as their employees.

The vast amounts of silver produced by the mines boosted the wealth of the Spanish government. Silver bullion (in the form of blocks) was sent back to Spain on treasure ships. Of the silver that arrived back in Spain, 25 per cent went direct to the Spanish treasury.

The Spanish government had to find a way of directly controlling its colonies in the New World as a means of ensuring that it got its share of the wealth being generated.

Now try this

Explain **two** consequences for Spain of the discovery of silver in the Spanish Empire.

Had a look ☐   Nearly there ☐   Nailed it! ☐   Expansion of empire

Governing the empire

The New World was conquered for Spain by the conquistadors but the Spanish government had to find a way of governing this newly won territory effectively.

How to govern the New World
- Find a way to govern the discovered territories and restore peace and stability.
- Make sure there is enough food and water.
- Put laws in place.
- Set up systems to manage daily life.
- Reward the conquistadors and their supporters with land and treasure.
- Ensure the conquistadors don't squabble among themselves.

The role of the viceroys
- The Council of the Indies appointed viceroys to govern Spanish territories.
- There were two viceroys: one in Mexico City and one in Lima (the viceroy of Peru).
- Viceroys were often military men but could also be churchmen or lawyers.
- They had great power as they acted on behalf of the Spanish government.
- Poor communications meant decisions took eight months to be approved.
- They governed through *cabildos* (town councils), which managed daily life.
- Justice was managed through the *audiencias* (courts), with judges who were independent of the viceroys.

Bartolome de las Casas
- ✓ Las Casas was a priest who travelled to the New World in 1512; he was given an *encomienda* in Cuba, where he witnessed the brutality of the conquistadors.
- ✓ He was made 'Protector of the Indians' and, in 1527, wrote a book, *A Short Account of the Destruction of the Indies*, describing the atrocities he had seen.
- ✓ In 1542 he persuaded Charles I to sign the New Laws to improve natives' lives.

The role of the *encomienda* system
- The system had already been set up in the West Indies and Mexico but was now imposed officially across the Spanish Empire.

> See also page 8 for how the *encomienda* system worked in practice.

- A Spaniard, often a conquistador, was allocated land and workers by the Spanish government, and became an *encomendero*.
- They could demand tribute from the native people on their estate but had to ensure that they were not exploited.
- They also had to pay for Catholic priests and monks to convert the natives to Christianity and provide and pay for the defence of the area with other *encomenderos*.

The New Laws
- It was made illegal to enslave natives.
- The amount of tribute that could be collected was limited.
- *Encomiendas* had to be passed back to the Spanish government on the death of an *encomendero* (landowner).

The significance of the New Laws, 1542
- The laws were intended to improve the rights of native people, but *encomenderos* opposed them and the viceroy of Peru refused to implement them.
- This led to revolts in Peru: the most serious (1544) had to be put down by the Spanish government and led to a temporary halt in the Spanish conquest of the New World in 1550.
- Though forced to suspend the New Laws, Charles I insisted that *encomiendas* be passed back to the Crown on the death of an *encomendero*, with royal agents in charge. The agents continued to exploit the native people, against the wishes of Las Casas.

Now try this

In a short paragraph, summarise how the role of viceroys helped Spain to govern its empire in the New World.

The foundation of La Paz, 1548

The city of La Paz, founded in 1548, became the administrative centre of the Spanish Empire.

Conquistador revolt in Peru, 1544

- The New Laws were unpopular among the *encomenderos* as they reduced their power and took away the right to pass on their land to heirs.
- This led to a serious revolt in Peru led by Gonzalo Pizarro, brother of Francisco Pizarro.

> Look back at pages 17–19 to revise Francisco Pizarro's conquest of Peru.

- The rebellion was initially successful and Gonzalo was able to rule the Inca territory for two years.
- However, the arrival of a Spanish army resulted in his execution and the restoration of Spanish authority.
- The revolt posed a problem about how Spain could govern its territories and control the rebellious *encomenderos* and conquistadors. This led to the founding of La Paz in 1548.

The capture of Gonzalo Pizarro in 1546. He was executed for treason in 1548.

The founding of La Paz

- The city of La Paz (in English 'The Peace'), in modern-day Bolivia, was founded in 1548 on the site of the Inca city of Laja.
- It was founded to commemorate the ending of Pizarro's revolt and to demonstrate that Spain was the highest authority, not the conquistadors.
- The city became the administrative centre of the Spanish Empire, with public buildings, churches and a street plan.
- The Spanish viceroy was based here, as were the *audiencias* (courts).
- The city was founded close to the trade routes near the Potosi and Oruro mines and this safeguarded Spanish control over the extraction of silver and trade. This ensured that silver continued to flow back to the Spanish government.
- Its location high up in the Andes made the city less vulnerable to attack.
- The establishment of the city represented the peak of conquistador conquest.

> In the Valladolid debate (1550), the Spanish priest Bartolome de las Casas was able to persuade Charles I to call a halt (temporarily) to the further conquest of the Americas.

> See page 21 for more about Las Casas.

Now try this

In **two** short paragraphs, explain the significance of Gonzalo Pizarro's revolt in 1544.

Had a look ☐   Nearly there ☐   Nailed it! ☐

Impact of the New World

Silver and gold

Silver, and some gold, was used to make coins and played an important role in enabling Spain to trade with the wider world.

Spanish trade routes, 1500–1600

The Spanish treasure route
- Vast amounts of silver were transported to Spain from the 1520s onwards.
- Ships often sailed the same routes to catch the trade winds.
- Ships laden with silver moving to and from the New World sailed in small treasure fleets to provide security for each other and assist if they were attacked or if the weather turned bad.

The effect of silver on Spain's economy
- Of the treasure that arrived in Spain, about 75 per cent went to Spanish merchants and conquistadors, and the rest to the Spanish treasury.
- It was used to make new eight-sided coins known as 'pieces of eight' (*pesos*), which allowed extensive trade with other European countries.
- Demand for goods increased, enabling foreign traders to put up their prices.
- This led to inflation as Spanish merchants passed on price rises to ordinary people, many of whom demanded higher wages.
- The silver was vital to support Spain's European Empire, equipping soldiers to make war against France (1542–46) and providing ships to guard the treasure fleets.
- However, as Spain's economy was based on the looted silver, people did not have to make money in other ways, with the result that Spanish industries developed more slowly than in other European countries.

Attacks on treasure fleets, c1555
- Spanish ships or galleons were an attractive target for pirates and **privateers**.

> **Privateers** were ships funded by hostile governments and men with money (investors) to attack shipping. The 'loot' (profit) was divided between investors.

- Privateers had initially come from France and England and began attacking Spanish treasure ships in the 1520s. The attacks increased during the war between Spain and France (1542–46) and continued.
- To combat this, the Spanish developed fleets to travel together in convoys, protected by fighting ships called galleons. Two convoy systems were created: the *Tierra Firma*, which sailed to South America; and the *New Spain*, which sailed to Mexico.

Now try this

Summarise the reasons why silver was so important to the Spanish economy.

Impact of the New World

Had a look ☐   Nearly there ☐   Nailed it! ☐

The impact of trade

Spain's monopoly of trade with the New World led to the development of Seville as a port, and growing labour shortages led to an expansion of the slave trade.

The growth of Seville

- All goods imported to Europe from the New World were required to pass through Seville's *Casa de Contratacion* (House of Trade), where merchants paid taxes and duties on the goods traded.
- Merchants from all over Europe travelled to Seville to buy goods from the New World and bring goods to be sold in the New World.
- Trade involved plants (cotton and tobacco), crops (wheat) and animals (horses, pigs and cattle).
- This gave Spain, and in particular Seville, a monopoly over trade with the New World, making its merchants and traders extremely wealthy.
- Seville was about 100 km inland so ships had to travel up the River Guadalquivir before reaching the port – this was inconvenient but it made the port difficult to attack.

The growth of the *Consulado de Mercaderes*

- Spanish merchants demanded a say in the running of the *Casa de Contratacion*.
- They set up a merchants' guild, the *Consulado de Mercaderes*, and formed a monopoly, which enabled them to control most of the trade with the Spanish colonies and keep prices high.
- Their control of the economies of both Spain and the New World grew.

By 1555, Seville was Spain's main trade link to the New World.

Labour shortages

> The *encomienda* system, the growing trade in cotton and tobacco, and the silver mines all required large amounts of labour.

⬇

> The native population had fallen owing to early death from diseases (including smallpox), overwork in silver mines, and mass killings in the early days of conquest.

⬇

> This resulted in labour shortages by the mid-1550s.

⬇

> The growing labour shortage started to lead to rising wages.

The growth of the slave trade

- Bartolome de las Casas was already suggesting in the 1520s that native labour could be replaced by African slaves, but later changed his mind.
- Under the Treaty of Tordesillas, the Spanish could not directly acquire slaves from West Africa as the Portuguese controlled the slave trade there.
- Spanish merchants were granted licences (*asientos*) to supply slaves to the New World. The licences were sold to the highest bidder. Those who bought them could buy slaves from the Portuguese and sell those slaves on to merchants in the New World for high prices. These slaves were then sold on to the *encomenderos*.

Now try this

Give **two** reasons why Seville emerged as one of the wealthiest cities in Europe by 1550.

Had a look ☐   Nearly there ☐   Nailed it! ☐

Impact of the New World

The government of the New World

A system of government, based in Castile, Spain, was developed to govern the New World. The role of the *Casa de Contratacion* and the Council of the Indies was to regulate trade.

The role of the (Casa de Contratacion) House of Trade

- It collected all colonial taxes and duties. A 20 per cent tax was charged on precious metals (the 'royal fifth'). Taxes were higher if naval protection was required for trading ships, and lower where investment was needed in the New World.
- The *Casa* was established in 1503 by Queen Isabella.
- It also licensed captains of ships with many attending a navigation school based in Seville, and administered the rules of business (commercial law).
- In theory, no Spaniard could sail anywhere without the approval of the *Casa*.
- It approved all voyages of exploration and trade and maintained secret information on trade routes and new discoveries of land. This secret map (known as the *Padrón Real*) was first drawn up in 1508 and updated as new land was discovered.

The *Casa* provided the Spanish treasury with income, enabling it to pay for wars with other European countries, including France. It created a trade monopoly with the New World. This kept prices high, allowing Spanish merchants to become very wealthy.

A version of the *Padrón Real* from 1529

The Council of the Indies

- The Council of the Indies was formed in 1524.
- It was based in Spain and consisted of a president and eight councillors.
- It controlled all matters that involved the New World.
- Members would discuss the messages or despatches received from viceroys in the New World, review them and make recommendations to the king as to what action should be taken in the parts of the New World controlled by Spain.
- Once a royal decision was made, it would be sent back to the Council of the Indies, and from the Council to the viceroys in the different parts of the Spanish New World. In this way, the Spanish government tried to exercise control over its empire in the New World. In practice, this was very difficult as time delays meant that it could be months before despatches were read and decisions taken. Real power therefore often rested with the viceroys who were 'the men on the spot' in the New World.

See page 21 for more on the role of the viceroys.

Now try this

Explain the ways in which the *Casa de Contratacion* helped to create a trade monopoly with the New World.

Skills | Had a look ☐ Nearly there ☐ Nailed it! ☐

Exam overview

This page introduces you to the main features and requirements of the Paper 2, Option P1 exam paper.

About Paper 2

- Paper 2 is for both your period study and your British depth study.
- Spain and the 'New World', c1490–1555 is a period study.
- You will answer all the questions in this option. In Question 3 you will pick two statements to explain out of a choice of three.

The Paper 2 exam lasts for 1 hour 45 minutes (105 minutes) in total. There are 32 marks for this period study and 32 marks for the British depth study, so you should spend about 50 minutes on each.

Remember to read each question carefully before you start to answer it.

The three questions

The three questions for Spain and the 'New World' will always follow this pattern.

Question 1
Explain **two** consequences of...   **(8 marks)**

Question 1 targets both AO1 and AO2. These questions focus on consequences – things that happened as a result of something.

Four of these marks are for Assessment Objective 2 (AO2). This is where you explain and analyse key events using historical concepts, which in this case is consequence.

Four of these marks are for Assessment Objective 1 (AO1). This is where you show your knowledge and understanding of the key features and characteristics of the period.

Question 2
Write a narrative account analysing...
Two prompts and your own information.
        (8 marks)

Question 2 also targets both AO1 and AO2. It asks you to provide an analytical narrative – an analysis of causation, consequence or change.

Question 3
Explain **two** of the following...
Three statements each starting:
The importance of... for...   **(16 marks)**

Question 3 targets both AO1 and AO2 and asks you to provide an analysis of consequence and significance – 'how important'.

You can see examples of all three questions on pages 27–32 of this Skills section, and in the Practice section on pages 33–42.

26

Had a look ☐ Nearly there ☐ Nailed it! ☐   Skills

Question 1: Explaining consequences 1

Question 1 on your exam paper will ask you to 'Explain **two** consequences of...'. There are 8 marks available for this question: 4 for each consequence.

Worked example

Explain **two** consequences of the conquest of Cuba (1514).   **(8 marks)**

 You can revise the conquest of Cuba on page 11.

What is a consequence?

A consequence is something that happens as a result of an event.

Help yourself to 'think consequences' by using phrases such as:

 As a result of...
 This meant that...
 This allowed...
 This led to...

Sample answer

Consequence 1:
Natives were massacred.

Consequence 2:
The Spanish wanted to conquer the island and add it to the Spanish Empire.

 This is a correct consequence of the conquest of Cuba, but make sure your answer explains why it was a consequence (AO2) or adds specific information to support the answer (AO1).

 This is not a consequence but a **reason for** the conquest of Cuba. Remember: for Section A of the exam it is essential to think **results of**, not reasons for.

Improved answer

Consequence 1:
The conquest resulted in the massacres of native communities. For example, at Caonao in 1513 around 2000 native people were slaughtered by the Spanish, who ran wild in the village.

Consequence 2:
The conquest also resulted in a decline in the native population of Cuba. There were an estimated 350 000 in 1514. This had fallen to about 3000 in 1555 as a result of slavery, massacre and disease, especially measles and smallpox.

You need to explain how the consequence of massacres resulted from the conquest, and also include relevant information from the period to support your answer: in this case, the massacre at Caonao.

 Note how the student has changed this from an explanation of an aim into the analysis of a consequence. Notice how the student has used the phrase 'as a result of...' to focus the answer on consequences. Make sure your answer explains how the conquest of Cuba led to these consequences.

27

Skills — Had a look ☐   Nearly there ☐   Nailed it! ☐

Question 1: Explaining consequences 2

Read carefully through this second Question 1 example and the student answers. The hints and tips on this page apply to all Question 1 questions, as do the ones on the previous page.

Worked example

Explain **two** consequences of the Spanish conquest of Mexico. **(8 marks)**

> **Explaining consequences**
> Consequences = results of.
> For consequences, think: 'what happened as a result of...?'
> To explain consequences, you must show the **connection** between the key event and the consequence.

🔗 **Links** You can revise the Spanish conquest of Mexico on pages 13–16.

Sample answer

Consequence 1:
The Aztecs were forced to convert to Christianity.

Consequence 2:
Spanish settlers were encouraged to arrive from Spain and Cuba. They were given land under the *encomienda* system.

→ This is a correct consequence but the student has only given a vague answer. Make sure you explain the consequence in your answer.

→ Notice how this is also a correct consequence and the beginning of an explanation: you would need to add more detail to the explanation to improve this answer.

Improved answer

Consequence 1:
The conquest of Mexico resulted in religious change. The Aztec religion was seen as blasphemous by the Spanish and it was abolished. Its priests were executed and religious icons destroyed. The Aztecs and other native people were required to convert to Christianity. Many did so outwardly, allowing themselves to be baptised as Christians and attending Mass. However, in private many continued to worship their old gods.

Consequence 2:
Another consequence of the conquest of Mexico was colonisation. Many of the conquistadors as well as other Spanish settlers from Spain and Cuba were given land holdings, or *encomiendas*, in Mexico. This meant that they became landowners and collected tribute from the native people, who were reduced to being farm workers and became virtual slaves. In this way a hierarchical society was established, with the Spanish *encomenderos* at the top and the native people at the bottom.

→ You should identify what the situation was like **before** the introduction of Christianity, as this will help you to explain the consequence that followed its introduction.

→ State the consequence and **explain** how that consequence resulted from the Spanish conquest of Mexico.

→ Use your knowledge of the period to support your answer.

🔗 **Links** The information about the *encomiendas* is useful for providing context. You can revise the *encomienda* system on page 21.

→ You can say 'Another consequence of this...' to make your answer clear.

→ You could also include some information about language change and how Spanish now became the main language in Mexico.

28

Had a look ☐ Nearly there ☐ Nailed it! ☐   Skills

Question 2: Analytical narrative 1

Question 2 on your exam paper will ask you to 'Write a narrative account analysing…'. A narrative account explains how events led to an outcome. There are 8 marks available for this question.

Worked example

Write a narrative account analysing the key events of 1532 and 1537 that led to the conquest of Peru. You may use the following in your answer:
- the death of Atahuallpa (1533)
- the siege of Cuzco (1536–37)

You **must** also use information of your own.

(8 marks)

 Links You can revise the conquest of Peru on pages 17–19.

Sample answer

The arrival of Pizarro in Peru in 1532 coincided with the death of Huayna Capac. He left the empire to his two sons, Atahuallpa and Huascar, who divided the empire between them. Atahuallpa got the northern half and Huascar the southern half. Because the nation was divided and many people had been killed or died from disease, Pizarro had an opportunity to seize power by attacking the Inca Empire when it was weak. Some native people were prepared to ally with the Spanish against Atahuallpa.

Pizarro approached Atahuallpa's camp and refused Inca hospitality. He agreed to meet and negotiate with Atahuallpa at Cajamarca town square, but instead Atahuallpa was accused of blasphemy and, with his army ambushed at the battle of Cajamarca, captured and ransomed for a room full of gold and double the amount of silver. When the ransom was paid Pizarro accused Atahuallpa of treason and publicly executed him. Pizarro then placed Manco, a younger son of Huayna Capac, on the throne, as a puppet king who would rule on behalf of the Spanish.

This led to the Inca revolt of 1536–37: Manco assembled an Inca army and attacked the Spanish and their native allies. At Cuzco, the capital of the Inca Empire, the Spanish and their native allies were besieged by the Inca army. The relief of the siege by other Spanish forces led to Manco withdrawing and establishing a separate state. This left Pizarro in control of Peru by 1537.

Analytical narrative

A narrative sounds like it means 'tell the story of…', but this is **not** what you need to do for this type of question.

The 'analytical' bit means you have to consider how key events were connected. Like all the questions in this paper, you need to think about **consequences** and **causes**: what happened as a result of a key event.

Key events

Your first step in writing an analytical narrative is to identify the key events in your narrative. This answer has selected the death of Huayna Capac, the battle of Cajamarca, the death of Atahuallpa and the siege of Cuzco.

Creating links

Once you have identified the key events, your answer should consider how one key event links to the next. This answer has signposted this with phrases such as 'Because…' and 'This led to…'.

Information of your own

The question states that you may use the two prompts it provides (the two bullet points) but also that 'you **must** also use information of your own'. Make sure you do use your own information; the best answers do this. In this answer the student has included their own information about Manco and the death of Huayna Capac.

Logical structure

If you plan your answer by noting down the key events first on scrap paper, this will help you structure your answer into a clear and logical sequence. Start with the earliest key event and work from one event to the next, identifying consequences, causes and changes.

Skills   Had a look ☐   Nearly there ☐   Nailed it! ☐

Question 2: Analytical narrative 2

Read carefully through this second Question 2 example and the student answers. The hints and tips on this page apply to all Question 2 questions, as do the ones on the previous page.

Worked example

Write a narrative account analysing the key events that led to the Treaty of Tordesillas (1494).
You may use the following in your answer:
- Columbus's discovery of the New World (1492)
- Portuguese claims to the New World (1493)

You **must** also use information of your own.

(8 marks)

More on analytical narrative

Question 2 asks you to explain how events led to an outcome. Identifying the events that were involved and showing how they led to the outcome provides the analysis. Showing how one event led to another event or was linked to existing circumstances provides the narrative. That's what makes it an analytical narrative.

 **Links** You can revise the Treaty of Tordesillas on page 6.

Sample extract

Columbus had sailed for the New World in 1492 on the understanding that any lands discovered would be given to Spain, although he would be given the title of Grand Admiral of the Ocean Sea. When Columbus returned, King John of Portugal also claimed lands in the New World under the Treaty of Alcacovas of 1479.

Notice how this answer extract relates to the prompt points in the question: Columbus's discovery of the New World and Portuguese claims to the New World.

Instead of providing an analytical narrative, this is a jumble of points about both prompts. Remember: you need to **identify the key events** that led to the outcome (the Treaty of Tordesillas) and then **link them together** in a **logical sequence**.

Improved extract

When Columbus landed in the Caribbean in 1492 he claimed the territories he discovered for Spain, as part of his sponsorship by Ferdinand and Isabella. This led to a dispute between Spain and Portugal on Columbus's return to Europe in 1493: King John of Portugal claimed that under the Treaty of Alcacovas (1479) the land belonged to Portugal because Portugal had, under this treaty, been given control of all lands to the west.

This dispute led to the possibility of war as Ferdinand and Isabella rejected Portugal's claim and began to assemble a fleet of ships in southern Spain close to Portugal.

As a result of this, Pope Alexander VI, wishing to avoid a war between two Christian monarchs, mediated in the dispute.

Note how the answer is set out in chronological order. This sequence makes it much easier to show how each key event links to the next.

The student has used their own knowledge to identify why Portugal claimed the land discovered by Columbus. Using your own knowledge in this way will help your analysis.

The answer selects good key events for its analytical narrative, and the student has made use of 'process' words and phrases. Remember to use these to show how one event led to another; for example: '**This dispute led to** the possibility of war as Ferdinand and Isabella rejected Portugal's claim... **As a result of this**, Pope Alexander VI, wishing to avoid a war...'

30

Had a look ☐   Nearly there ☐   Nailed it! ☐   Skills

Question 3: Explaining importance 1

Question 3 provides three statements about the **importance** of events and developments, and asks you to pick two of them and **explain** why they were important. There are 16 marks available for this question: 8 marks for each explanation.

Worked example

Explain **two** of the following:

- [X] The importance of the New Laws for the government of the Spanish Empire.
- [ ] The importance of the voyage of Magellan for the growth of the Spanish Empire.
- [ ] The importance of the capture of Tenochtitlan for the defeat of the Aztecs.

(16 marks)

Choosing which point to answer

Although three bullet points are listed, the question only asks you to pick **two** of them for your answer: you should pick the two you can answer best and write two separate answers for this question.

Pay careful attention to exactly what you are being asked to explain: the second part of each bullet point gives you the specific focus of the question.

On the exam paper, put a cross in the box to show which question you are answering. The answer extract below is for the first part of the first question.

Links You can revise these events on pages 12, 14 and 21.

Sample extract

The New Laws were passed in 1542. They made it illegal for slaves to be forced to work if they did not want to and forbade the capturing of natives so that they could work as slaves. The New Laws also limited the tribute collected from natives and stated that *encomiendas* had to be passed back to the Spanish government on the death of an *encomendero*.

Although the student includes accurate and relevant detail about the New Laws, notice how they do not show any analysis of their importance. When answering a question like this, think first about the reasons why the New Laws changed the government of the Spanish Empire, and then use your knowledge about the period to support your analysis.

The best answers show analysis of importance (AO2) together with detail (AO1).

In order to improve their answer, the student spent two minutes planning their response before they started to write it. This is what they did:

The New Laws
- Enhanced the rights of the natives
- Limited the powers of the encomenderos
- Revolts were put down but New Laws abandoned = failure of the New Laws
- Were opposed by royal officials including the Viceroy of Peru, who refused to implement them

Planning your answer makes a lot of sense because it helps you focus on the demands of the question. Also, you can structure your answer and it helps you plan your time. But make sure it is a **quick** plan that allows you plenty of time to write your answer.

You can see part of the improved answer that the student wrote using this plan on the next page.

Don't forget that you need to write answers for **two** parts of the question!

Skills | Had a look ☐ | Nearly there ☐ | Nailed it! ☐

Question 3: Explaining importance 2

This student answer is an improved version of the student answer from the previous page. The hints and tips on this page apply to all Question 3 questions, as do the ones on the previous page.

Worked example

Explain **two** of the following:
- [X] The importance of the New Laws for the government of the Spanish Empire.
- [ ] The importance of the voyage of Magellan for the growth of the Spanish Empire.
- [ ] The importance of the capture of Tenochtitlan for the defeat of the Aztecs.

(16 marks)

Importance and significance

Question 3 tests your ability to explain how and why an event is significant. A strong answer would explain two or three consequences of the event and contain relevant factual knowledge. The best answers will also be organised and flow smoothly, something you can achieve by using 'linking' phrases such as 'It was also important because it led to...' or 'Thirdly, it meant that...'.

Links You can revise these events on pages 12, 14 and 21.

Improved extract

The New Laws were important because they strengthened Spanish control of the New World, reduced the powers of *encomenderos* and enhanced the rights of the natives. This resulted in a revolt in 1544 and the Laws were suspended.

Spanish control of the New World was strengthened under the Laws because *encomiendas* had to be passed back to the Spanish government on the death of an *encomendero*. This increased Spanish control as the Spanish government, through the Council of the Indies, could control who inherited the *encomiendas*, forcing Spanish conquistadors and merchants to be obedient if they wanted to keep these estates.

The Laws also increased the rights of the natives and reduced the power of the *encomenderos*: natives could no longer be captured and forced to work as slaves and the amount that the *encomenderos* could collect as tribute from the natives was limited, reducing their power and wealth.

This resulted in a revolt by the *encomenderos*, backed by the Viceroy of Peru, which had to be put down by Spanish troops in 1546. Most of the laws were suspended, although *encomiendas* still returned to the Spanish government on the death of *encomenderos*. The suspension meant that the rights of native people remained unprotected and Spanish colonists continued to exploit them.

The student has used their plan (see previous page) to structure their answer. Notice how the student often starts a new paragraph when moving on to a new reason why the New Laws were important.

The student backs up the reason why the Laws were important with specific information. For example, here it is the information about how landholdings had to be passed back to the Spanish government on the death of an *encomendero*.

It is easy, when writing answers to questions like this, to start to drift away from the event in the question (the New Laws) and talk about the laws in general. Notice how the student does not do that – the focus stays on the New Laws and their importance.

Notice how the student again uses relevant information to support their points here.

It is useful to link the importance of the New Laws with other events that were factors in the development of Spanish government in the New World: the revolt of 1544 in this case.

The student has tried to link the points together and has developed them throughout, using evidence to support their reasoning.

Had a go ☐   Nearly there ☐   Nailed it! ☐

Practice

Practice

Put your skills and knowledge into practice with the following question.

Option P1: Spain and the 'New World', c1490–c1555

1 Explain **two** consequences of the voyage of Magellan (1519–22). **(8 marks)**

Consequence 1:

Guided One consequence of Magellan's voyage was that it opened up the Pacific, leading to further exploration and Magellan's claiming of the Philippines for Spain in 1521.

Consequence 2:

You have 1 hour 45 minutes for the **whole** of Paper 2, so you should spend about **50 minutes** on this option: Spain and the 'New World', c1490–c1555. Remember to leave five minutes or so to check your work when you've finished writing.

Links You can revise the voyage of Magellan on page 12.

You need to identify **two** valid consequences and support each one.

To support the first consequence here, you need to show how Magellan's voyage led to his claiming of the Philippines for Spain, and what this meant for the Spanish Empire.

Your exam paper will have a separate space for each consequence you need to explain.

Remember to include **two** consequences in your answer and to spend equal time on both.

Practice

Had a go ☐   Nearly there ☐   Nailed it! ☐

Practice

Put your skills and knowledge into practice with the following question.

2 Write a narrative account analysing the key events of 1484–92 that led to Columbus's first voyage to the New World.

You may use the following in your answer:
- Ferdinand and Isabella's funding of Columbus's expedition (1491).
- The conquest of Granada (1492)

You **must** also use information of your own. **(8 marks)**

It is a good idea to plan your answer quickly first by making a list of relevant key events in the period covered by the question. For example:

1480s – Columbus petitions European kings to support his voyage financially

1490 – growing belief that there were lands to the west of Spain, including the Indies

1491 – Spain backs Columbus's proposed voyage

1492 – Conquest of Granada

This gives you a structure for your answer.

Links You can revise events leading up to Columbus's voyage on pages 1–2.

It is very important to bring information of your own into your answer, in order to make it as strong as possible.

Remember to analyse the links between the events and support this with relevant information. You can highlight that you are making connections with phrases such as: 'because of this…'; 'as a result of…'; 'this led to…'. Your analysis can look at causation, consequence and change.

Had a go ☐   **Nearly there** ☐   **Nailed it!** ☐

Practice

Use this page to continue your answer to Question 2.

> Remember, this is not a question about Columbus's voyage but about **the events leading up to it**. For example, Columbus's need for financial support, the role of the Church and the willingness of Ferdinand and Isabella to support his expedition. How did these lead to Columbus's voyage?

> Your answer should set out a clear sequence of events that leads to an outcome. In this case, the outcome is Columbus's first voyage to the New World in 1492.

> Make sure you only cover the range of years given in the question: 1484–92. This is not a question where you can use your knowledge of Columbus's actual voyage to the New World (1492–93).

> Make sure you support your analysis with a good range of accurate and relevant detail throughout your answer.

Practice   Had a go ☐   Nearly there ☐   Nailed it! ☐

Practice

Put your skills and knowledge into practice with the following question.

> 3 Explain **two** of the following:
> - ☐ i The importance of the discovery of silver in Bolivia and Mexico for the Spanish government. **(8 marks)**
> - ☐ ii The importance of Cortes's time as governor and captain-general of New Spain for the Aztecs. **(8 marks)**
> - ☐ iii The importance of Pizarro's expedition of 1526–27 for the growth of the Spanish Empire. **(8 marks)**
>
> **(Total for Question 3 = 16 marks)**

*Although three events are listed, the question only asks you to pick **two** of them for your answer: you should pick the two you can answer best and write two separate answers.*

Pay careful attention to what exactly you are being asked to explain: the second part of each event gives you the specific focus of the question.

Write a sentence defining your event and then at least two paragraphs explaining its importance. Remember to include enough detail in your answer and try to link your consequences together.

If you decide to answer Question 3(i) turn to page 37. If you decide to answer Question 3(ii), turn to page 39. If you decide to answer Question 3(iii), turn to page 41.

🔗 **Links** You can revise the importance of the discovery of silver in Bolivia and Mexico for the Spanish government on page 20. For more about the importance of Cortes's time as governor and captain-general of New Spain for the Aztecs, turn to page 16. Find out more about the importance of Pizarro's second voyage (1526–27) for the growth of the Spanish Empire on page 17.

Answering the question

On the exam paper you will see exam Question 3 on one page and then you'll turn onto a new page to start your answer to your first choice of question.

In the exam you will have two full pages of paper for each of the two questions that you choose to do.

You should spend about 12 minutes answering each of the questions you have chosen.

Had a go ☐   Nearly there ☐   Nailed it! ☐   Practice

Practice

Put your skills and knowledge into practice with the following question.

Indicate which question you are answering by marking a cross in the box ☒. If you change your mind, put a line through the box ~~☒~~ and then indicate your new question with a cross ☒.

- ☒ **i** The importance of the discovery of silver in Bolivia and Mexico for the Spanish government.
- ☐ **ii** The importance of Cortes's reign as governor and captain-general of New Spain for the Aztecs.
- ☐ **iii** The importance of Pizarro's expedition of 1526–27 for the growth of the Spanish Empire.

....
....
....
....
....
....
....
....
....
....
....
....
....
....
....
....
....
....
....
....
....

> You can show which question you will answer first by putting a cross in the box next to that question. That saves a lot of time as you don't need to write the question out! If you put a cross next to the wrong question by mistake, don't worry. Just put a line through the cross and put a cross next to the question you have chosen to answer.

> Question 3 is testing your ability to explain how and why an event is significant for a particular development. That means talking about consequences. For example, 'the discovery of silver in Bolivia and Mexico was **important for the Spanish government because** the treasury received 25 per cent of the silver bullion that arrived back in Spain. **This made the Spanish government very wealthy, which allowed it to build up its army and navy. In turn, this enabled Spain to expand its empire and** fight a war against France between 1542 and 1546.'
> - Link to question
> - Shows analysis
> - Consequence
> - AO1 information

> A strong answer would explain two or three consequences of the event that show its importance and contain relevant factual knowledge. For example, the need to transport silver bullion back to Spain led to the growth of treasure fleets and convoys, including the *Tierra Firme* and the *New Spain*.

37

Practice

Had a go ☐ Nearly there ☐ Nailed it! ☐

Practice

Use this space to continue your answer to Question 3(i) if necessary.

....

> Remember: you need to write about the **importance** of the discovery of silver in Mexico and Bolivia for the Spanish government. Don't just describe what happened.

> You don't have to write a formal conclusion, but a sentence or two summarising or briefly explaining your key points might help here. For example, you could say: 'The discovery of silver in Bolivia and Mexico boosted the wealth of the Spanish government, enabling it to expand its empire further. It also forced it to introduce a convoy system to enable the silver bullion to be transported safely to Spain.'

> Make sure you support your explanation with a good range of accurate and relevant detail throughout your answer.

Had a go ☐   Nearly there ☐   Nailed it! ☐   Practice

Practice

Put your skills and knowledge into practice with the following question.

Indicate which question you are answering by marking a cross in the box ☒. If you change your mind, put a line through the box ☒ and then indicate your new question with a cross ☒.

- ☐ i The importance of the discovery of silver in Bolivia and Mexico for the Spanish government.
- ☒ ii The importance of Cortes's time as governor and captain-general of New Spain for the Aztecs.
- ☐ iii The importance of Pizarro's expedition of 1526–27 for the growth of the Spanish Empire.

> When you start your second answer to Question 3, you again show which question you are answering by putting a cross next to that question. You don't have to answer the questions in the order in which they are presented.

> Although there are equal marks for AO1 and AO2, it's particularly important to focus on AO2 and remember to analyse **importance**. The best answers do this.

> Using words to indicate consequences and significance will help you keep your AO2 focus. For example: 'Cortes's time as governor and captain-general was **important because** it changed Aztec religious practices.'

Practice

Had a go ☐   Nearly there ☐   Nailed it! ☐

Practice

Use this space to continue your answer to Question 3(ii) if necessary.

> The mark scheme for Question 3 says that the best answers:
> - show analysis of importance (AO2)
> - have a clear structure so it is easy to follow the analysis (AO2)
> - include accurate and relevant information (AO1)
> - show good knowledge and understanding of the period (AO1).

> Remember to use your AO1 information to back up your analysis. For example, you could say: 'Before the Spanish conquest the Aztecs practised a religion based on human sacrifice to their gods, who would in turn ensure that there was a good harvest. The Catholic Church saw this as blasphemous. As a result, the Spanish killed many of the Aztec priests and noblemen, and Aztec people were required to convert to Christianity.'

Had a go ☐   Nearly there ☐   Nailed it! ☐   Practice

Practice

Put your skills and knowledge into practice with the following question.

Indicate which question you are answering by marking a cross in the box ☒. If you change your mind, put a line through the box ☒ and then indicate your new question with a cross ☒.

- ☐ i The importance of the discovery of silver in Bolivia and Mexico for the Spanish government.
- ☐ ii The importance of Cortes's reign as governor and captain-general of New Spain for the Aztecs.
- ☒ iii The importance of Pizarro's expedition of 1526–27 for the growth of the Spanish Empire.

....
....
....
....
....
....
....
....
....
....
....
....
....
....
....
....
....
....
....
....
....

When you start your second answer to Question 3, you again show which question you are answering by putting a cross next to that question. You don't have to answer the questions in the order in which they are presented.

Although there are equal marks for AO1 and AO2, it's particularly important to focus on AO2 and remember to analyse importance. The best answers do this.

*Using words to indicate consequences and significance will help you keep your AO2 focus. For example: 'Pizarro's expedition of 1526–27 **brought about**...'*

Remember: you are looking at how important Pizarro's expedition of 1526–27 was for the growth of the Spanish Empire. What did it lead to? Did the Spanish Empire expand as a result of this expedition?

For each point you make, always then explain how it relates to the question.

Practice

Had a go ☐ Nearly there ☐ Nailed it! ☐

Practice

Use this space to continue your answer to Question 3(iii) if necessary.

> The mark scheme for Question 3 says that the best answers:
> - show analysis of importance (AO2)
> - have a clear structure so it is easy to follow the analysis (AO2)
> - include accurate and relevant information (AO1)
> - show good knowledge and understanding of the period (AO1).

> Your accurate and relevant information could include points such as: 'Pizarro's expedition of 1526–27 demonstrated that the Inca Empire in South America was large and wealthy.'

> Remember to use your AO1 information to back up your analysis. For example, you could say: 'Pizarro's discoveries in his expedition of 1526–27 meant that he wanted to launch a further expedition to Peru. However, he was refused permission to do so by the governor of Panama, so he returned to Spain in 1528 to petition the king to approve an expedition to conquer Peru. This resulted in a licence called the *Capitulacion de Toledo* in July 1529, giving Pizarro permission to launch an expedition aimed at adding Peru to the Spanish Empire.'

Answers

Where an exemplar answer is given, this is not necessarily the only correct response. In most cases there is a range of responses that can gain full marks.

SUBJECT CONTENT

Spain reaches the 'New World', c1490–1512

Spanish exploration
1. Spain, c1490

Isabella was keen for Spain to participate in voyages of exploration and discovery owing to her personal piety and the 'crusading spirit'. Crusades aimed to convert people to Christianity in unknown lands. The Church approved of this, and the religious devotion of the people meant that many supported such voyages. Isabella believed that she would benefit spiritually if Spain funded these expeditions and also that it would demonstrate her piety, boosting her popularity. Crusades also justified the expansion of the Spanish Empire and the gaining of treasure, adding to the Spanish government's wealth.

2. Columbus and sponsorship

Any **one** of the following:

- A successful expedition would raise Spain's status ahead of Portugal as they, and not Portugal, could claim control over any lands Columbus discovered.
- The expedition, if successful, would provide great riches and income for the Spanish treasury, making the government rich. This would enable it to finance more expeditions elsewhere.
- Isabella, in particular, saw the expedition as an opportunity to spread Christianity to other lands. Her crusading zeal was an important reason for her support for Columbus.
- Isabella's personal priest and friend of Columbus, Juan Perez, supported the scheme and helped to put Columbus's case to Isabella.

3. Columbus's first voyage, 1492

Any **two** of the following:

- Columbus had to find ships that were large enough to travel on the open seas for long periods of time. Columbus solved this problem by finding three ships, the *Nina*, the *Pinta* and the *Santa Maria*. He also recruited two sailors, the Pinzon brothers, who could help captain and equip them.
- Columbus had to stock up with enough provisions. He ensured that he had enough provisions to last for at least a year. These included preserved food, wine and water as well as items to trade with native people in foreign lands.
- There was the possibility that the Portuguese might obstruct his voyage. Columbus adjusted his route to avoid this.
- Columbus had to address the fears of the crew, who were uneasy about sailing for long periods of time without sight of land. Columbus solved this problem by keeping two logs: an accurate log which he kept to himself, and one which he showed to the crew that understated the distance travelled.
- Columbus had a disagreement with Martin Pinzon, who wanted to sail southwards as he believed he would find Japan. Columbus solved this problem by persuading him to sail westwards.

Columbus and the Caribbean
4. The Bahamas and the Caribbean

Columbus constructed the fort because he was faced with a mutiny by the captain of the *Pinta*, Martin Pinzon, who left without permission to look for gold. Columbus experienced further difficulties when the *Santa Maria* ran aground. This forced Columbus to leave 39 men behind to look for gold while he returned to Spain on the *Nina*, in January 1493. They built a fort, La Navidad, to give the men somewhere to live.

La Navidad also protected the sailors from attack. There had already been trouble at Samana and there was a risk of further attacks.

5. Impact of contact with natives

The incident at Samana was important because it worsened the relationship between the Spanish and the native people. Columbus had been prepared to use force to take gold and make the expedition successful, but, at the same time, he viewed some of the natives as generally peaceful. After Samana, Columbus said that he wanted the native people to fear the Spanish.

6. Rivalry with Portugal

The intervention of Pope Alexander VI resolved the dispute between Portugal and Spain over the lands in the New World. Under the Treaty of Tordesillas, a line was drawn from the North Pole to the South Pole, 2000 kilometres to the west of Cape Verde. All lands to the west of this line were Spanish. All lands to the east, with the exception of the Canaries, were Portuguese. This meant that most of the New World was left to the Spanish, with only the eastern parts of South America being Portuguese. Africa was left to the Portuguese.

Spanish claims
7. Columbus's other voyages

1 In 1496, Columbus left the settlement at Isabela, placing his brother Bartholomew in charge. Bartholomew abandoned Isabela and set up a new colony at Santo Domingo.

In 1498, Columbus returned from Spain to find the settlement at Santo Domingo in uproar. Columbus was able to calm the revolt by offering the settlers some rights, including land and native labourers to work on it. However, discontent continued and Columbus responded by hanging several Spaniards and natives.

Columbus appealed to Ferdinand and Isabella and they sent their representative, Francisco de Bobadilla, to replace Columbus as governor. Bobadilla upheld the settlers' complaints and, in 1500, Columbus was taken back to Spain to face trial.

2   The revolt at Santo Domingo was important because it resulted in a confrontation between Columbus and the Spanish settlers. Columbus hanged some Spanish settlers and natives. The revolt exposed a clear rift between Columbus, who wanted to develop the New World as a colony by planting crops and clearing forests, and the settlers, who wanted to plunder as much gold and treasure as they could.

The revolt was also important because it resulted in Columbus no longer being governor. Columbus had appealed to Ferdinand and Isabella for support, but Francisco de Bobadilla, who was sent to resolve the matter, supported the settlers' grievances and sent Columbus back to Spain as a prisoner.

8. Effects of Spanish settlement

Any **two** of the following;
- The native people were forced to accept the *encomienda* system, under which Spanish settlers were allocated land inhabited by groups of native people. Natives had to give the Spanish goods or work without payment in the gold mines set up by the Spanish.
- The Spanish promised to protect the native people, teach them Spanish and convert them to Christianity, but in fact many were exploited by the Spanish.
- Many native people were hunted and captured as slaves before being sent to the slave markets in Spain. This policy was stopped by Isabella, who freed and returned some of them to the New World.
- Those who resisted slavery were treated brutally. They were often mutilated, burned alive or attacked by hunting dogs.
- The native population was devastated by disease, having no immunity to diseases such as smallpox and measles carried in by the Spanish from Europe.

9. Development of an imperial policy

The Laws of Burgos were significant because they defined the relationship between the Spanish settlers and the natives. The laws stated that the natives were to be treated kindly by the Spanish settlers and have their hours of work regulated, but they also upheld the *encomienda* system, which, in practice, meant the natives were often in a condition of slavery. The laws also allowed Spanish officials to punish natives who broke the laws. Significantly, the laws also required native people to give up their old religious practices and convert to Christianity.

The conquistadors, 1513–c1528

Start of an empire

10. Balboa and the conquistadors, 1513–28

Any **two** from:
- Balboa's expeditions in Central America were important because they led to the discovery of the Pacific. Balboa claimed the Pacific for Spain, increasing Spain's potential empire in the New World and beyond.
- They were also important because they were a starting point for further expeditions in Mexico (Cortes) and Peru (Pizarro) as well as the Pacific coast (Espinosa).
- The expeditions also led to the establishment of Panama as a Spanish colony.

11. The conquest of Cuba

By 1511, there was already an acute labour shortage in the Spanish-controlled areas of the New World. Death from illness had reduced the amount of slave labour available in Haiti and other islands already controlled by the Spanish.

To obtain more slaves and plunder the gold and silver of Cuba, Velazquez launched an invasion in 1511 and tried to capture a native chief, Hatuey, who along with 300 followers had already escaped from Haiti.

The conquest was violent. Hatuey was captured and burned to death, having refused to convert to Christianity. At Caonao in 1513 around 2000 native people were slaughtered by the Spanish, who ran amok in the village.

The rest of the island was then conquered by the Spanish by1514. All natives were required to convert to Christianity.

12. The voyage of Magellan

Any **one** of the following:
- The Spice Islands were a rich source of valuable spices, including mace, nutmeg and pepper. These could be exported to Europe and sold at an enormous profit. The Spanish discovery of the Spice Islands would mean that they would become part of the Spanish Empire and stop rival countries, including Portugal, from acquiring them.
- Claiming the islands for Spain would provide the Spanish with further trading opportunities as goods made in Spain and the New World could be sold there and spices bought there.
- Magellan's discovery of the islands would confirm that the East Indies could be reached by sailing westwards.

Conquest of Mexico

13. Expedition to Mexico, 1519

Any **two** of:
- Velázquez, the governor of Cuba, was very ambitious. He wanted the wealth and fame that would come from claiming more land for Spain, as well as to improve his position with the Church as a result of spreading Christianity.

- While working for Velazquez in Cuba, Cortes had become rich. He wanted to extend his power, wealth and influence by exploring Mexico.
- Reports of stone cities and beautiful gold and silver objects were very attractive to Cortes and he was willing to launch an expedition to Mexico to find them.

14. Key events of the conquest

For example, **one** of the following:

- The Tlaxcalans and others allied themselves with the Spanish, increasing the size of Cortes's army and enabling him to besiege the city.
- Cortes surrounded Tenochtitlan and starved the inhabitants, making it easier to attack and capture the city.

Spain's impact

15. Cortes's actions 1523–28

Any **two** of the following;

- Cortes rebuilt Tenochtitlan and renamed it Mexico City for Spain, destroying all Aztec religious temples.
- Cortes killed the Aztecs' political and religious leaders. This strengthened Spanish control by wiping out the Aztecs' rulers, leaving people leaderless and unable to challenge the Spanish.
- He gave land to the Spanish, encouraged others to settle there and set up the *encomienda* system. This strengthened Spanish control of the countryside.
- Spanish explorers were encouraged to launch expeditions to expand Spanish influence in Central America. Expeditions were sent to the main gold-producing region of Mexico, attracting other Spanish explorers to the region.
- Hundreds of Franciscan friars went out to New Spain from 1523 onwards, founded the Church in Mexico and converted thousands of native people.

16. Consequences for the Aztecs

Any **two** of the following;

- The Aztec ruling class were almost all killed. The position of the emperor was abolished and the Aztec nobility and priests were murdered. This weakened Aztec society by depriving it of leadership.
- The Aztec Empire now became 'New Spain' and part of a growing Spanish Empire in the New World. The Aztecs were now ruled by the Spanish, not by an Aztec ruler.
- The Aztec religion was abolished and the Aztecs forced to convert to Christianity. However, many still worshipped their old gods in private.
- The Spanish conquest resulted in diseases such as smallpox and measles, which significantly reduced the native population. The population of Mexico fell from 25 million (1519) to 6.2 million (1555).
- The Aztecs had to adopt Spanish as their main language. This meant that native languages became much less important after 1519. Many Aztecs became bilingual.
- The Aztecs were also affected by changes to farming, which changed their diet. The Spanish introduced meat and dairy farming as well as wheat and other cereals.
- The Aztecs were also affected by colonisation. Spanish settlers were encouraged to arrive from Spain and Cuba and were given land under the *encomienda* system. The Aztecs were reduced to virtual slaves and forced to pay tribute to the Spanish.
- Intermarriage took place between the Spanish and the Aztec population. By 1550 three groups existed: the Spanish settlers, the Mestizo (half Spanish/half native) and the original natives.
- Employment also changed. Many Aztecs had to work mining iron, gold and silver. Others worked in tobacco and cotton plantations.

17. Pizarro and Panama

Pizarro returned to Spain from his second expedition with evidence of Inca wealth, including llamas, silver and gold. He appealed to King Charles I, asking him to back a third expedition that would 'extend the empire of Castile'. Charles gave Pizarro a licence, the *Capitulacion de Toledo*, in July 1529, authorising him to conquer Peru.

The Spanish Empire, c1528–c1555

Conquest of the Incas

18. Pizarro's arrival in Peru

December 1530: Pizarro leaves Panama on his third expedition.

January 1531: Pizarro lands in Ecuador.

April 1532: Pizarro arrives in Peru.

April to November 1532: Pizarro approaches Atahuallpa's camp.

15 November 1532: Atahuallpa invites Pizarro to meet him in the town square at Cajamarca the next day.

16 November 1532: Spanish ambush results in the Battle of Cajamarca, where thousands of Incas are killed and Atahuallpa is taken prisoner.

19. Pizarro's conquest of Peru

- The Spanish had imprisoned Atahuallpa and demanded a large ransom, but when it was paid they broke their promise and killed Atahuallpa.
- The Spanish crowned Manco as emperor, but then treated him as a puppet king to rule on their behalf.

Expansion of empire

20. Discovery of silver in Bolivia and Mexico

Any **two** of the following:

- Mining created the need for vast amounts of labour to extract and smelt the silver ore. This led to the development of mining towns at Potosi, Guanajuato and Zacatecas, which developed quickly into towns housing miners and their families.

- The discovery of silver resulted in rumours and legends that there remained a vast amount of undiscovered wealth in the New World, including El Dorado, the so-called 'City of Gold' which was rumoured to exist somewhere in America.
- Many Spanish merchants invested in projects in the New World designed to explore the area further in the hope of finding more gold and silver. This led to expeditions to California, Venezuela and Argentina during the 16th century.
- There was increased settlement of the New World as the conquistadors were joined by other adventurers, merchants and speculators as well as those who worked for them.
- Silver mining boosted the wealth of the Spanish government, which claimed 25 per cent tax on the silver mined and shipped back to Spain in the form of silver bullion.
- The Spanish government had to find a way of directly controlling its colonies in the New World as a means of ensuring that it got its share of the wealth generated there.

21. Governing the empire

Viceroys in the New World were powerful as they governed on behalf of the Spanish government. The laws they passed affected both Spanish and native people. However, their power was limited by poor communications which meant that it could take eight months for their decisions to be implemented. Many day-to-day decisions were taken by local councils or *cabildos*.

22. The foundation of La Paz, 1548

The revolt was significant because it demonstrated the difficulties associated with governing Spain's empire in the New World. The revolt had taken place because many Spanish landowners opposed the New Laws and were not prepared to obey them. This created a need to establish a system of government that would enable Spain to control the more rebellious conquistadors, while protecting the silver bullion that was flowing into the treasury.

This led to the establishment of La Paz (in modern-day Bolivia) in 1548 as the main administrative centre of the Spanish Empire. The viceroy and the courts were based there. The city's position, close to the silver mines, ensured that the Spanish government kept control of the area's silver.

Impact of the New World

23. Silver and gold

Because the Spanish government and merchants had so much silver minted into silver coins, they were able to trade with other European countries. Traders in other countries put up their prices, and Spanish merchants passed on these price rises to ordinary people. As poorer people could not afford to buy goods, they demanded higher wages. This pushed up prices even more because it increased the production costs of goods made in Spain.

The silver was also vital to the Spanish government, which used it to pay and equip soldiers to make war against France (1542–46) as well as to provide ships to guard the treasure fleets returning to Spain from the New World.

24. The impact of trade

1 Spain enjoyed a monopoly of trade with the New World. This led to the growth of Seville as a port because all goods imported from the New World were required to stop there and pass through the city's *Casa de Contratacion* (House of Trade) where they paid taxes and duties on the goods traded.

2 Merchants from all over Europe travelled to Seville in order to buy goods from the New World and bring their own goods that they wanted to sell in the New World. This trade involved plants (cotton and tobacco), crops (wheat) and animals (horses, pigs and cattle). This gave Seville, in particular, a monopoly over trade with the New World, making its merchants and traders very rich.

25. The government of the New World

The *Casa de Contratacion* was set up to regulate trade with the New World. It approved all voyages of exploration and trade as well as licensing ships' captains. It also established the rules of business with the New World. This gave the Spanish government control over trade with the New World as merchants had to have its approval before sailing or trading there. This meant that Spain had a trade monopoly in the New World.

PRACTICE
33. Practice

1 There are 4 marks available for each consequence. The two consequences are each marked separately. If your answer doesn't include any analysis of why it is a consequence, then the most you can get for your answer is 2 marks.

Your consequences could include two of the following:

- It opened up the Pacific, leading to further exploration and Magellan claiming the Philippines for Spain in 1521. This meant that the Philippines became part of the Spanish Empire and that Spain's territory extended into the Pacific, enabling it to dominate world trade, as spices could be added to the gold and silver being exported from the New World.
- It established that the earth was round and that Columbus was right to believe that the East Indies could be reached by sailing westwards.

This encouraged further exploration and trade, especially in the northern Pacific and South East Asia during the later 1500s, involving England, Spain and Portugal. This increased tension and trade rivalry, especially between England and Spain.

- The opening up of the Pacific meant ships could also sail up the Pacific coast, allowing exploration and trade along the west coast of North America. This meant that by the mid-1540s areas such as California were incorporated into the Spanish Empire, expanding Spanish territory in the New World.

34. Practice

2 There are 8 marks on offer for this question: 4 marks for AO1 (knowledge and understanding) and 4 marks for AO2 (the analysis of consequence/cause/change). A level 1 answer would get 1 or 2 marks only because the answer would only have very limited analysis and only very limited knowledge and understanding of the events and would be poorly organised. A level 3 answer (6–8 marks) would be very well structured so there is a clear sequence of events that leads to an outcome. The account would analyse how the events are linked and this would all be supported by accurate and relevant information.

Points that you could make in your analytical narrative are as follows (highlighting shows where answers start to analyse consequences):

- By the 1490s there was a growing belief, thanks to the discovery of the Canaries and Madeira, that there were lands to the west of Spain across the Atlantic Ocean. Some even believed that this provided an alternative route to the Spice Islands of the East Indies. This would open up profitable trading opportunities for those able to establish a trade route by sea and control over any territories discovered and explored.

- This led to Columbus seeking to gain sponsorship in the 1480s for an expedition westwards across the Atlantic. He visited the French, Portuguese and English courts looking for financial support, but was unsuccessful.

- However, in 1491, the Spanish monarchs Ferdinand and Isabella were prepared to back an expedition. This was because of the 'crusading spirit' in Spain. Isabella, a devout Catholic, was about to complete the conquest of the Kingdom of Granada and saw an expedition as an opportunity to spread Christianity to distant lands and gain the approval of the Pope. In this regard the influence of Isabella's personal priest and friend of Columbus, Juan Perez, was important, as he backed the scheme and persuaded Isabella to support it. Ferdinand and Isabella also recognised the financial profits that would be made if the expedition was successful, as Spain would claim any lands discovered before Portugal.

- This meant that Columbus received support from Spain and was granted the title Grand Admiral of the Ocean Sea. He would be appointed governor of any newly colonised lands and would be entitled to 10 per cent of the produce of any territories discovered. He was also provided with the funds to hire three ships: the *Nina*, the *Pinta* and the *Santa Maria*, as well as the crews required to complete his voyage of exploration.

36. Practice

3 For Question 3, you pick two out of the three parts of the Question on offer, with each part being worth 8 marks for a total of 16. That makes Question 3 worth half of all the marks available for your Spain and the 'New World' exam, so it is important to leave yourself plenty of time for this question and to give equal time to each of the two parts you tackle. Since you cannot get any more than 8 marks for the first answer, it is not a good idea to spend all your Question 3 time on the first answer and not leave enough to do a good job on the second.

Notes for answers on all three of the parts are provided here, but do remember that you only need to answer two.

(i) An answer about why the discovery of silver in Bolivia and Mexico was important for the Spanish government might include these points:

- The discovery of silver was important to the growth of the Spanish Empire. Of the bullion that arrived back in Spain, 25 per cent went straight to the Spanish treasury. In addition, the government charged a 20 per cent tax on precious metals, known as the 'royal fifth'. This increased the wealth of the Spanish government as large amounts of silver made their way back across the Atlantic on treasure ships. The risk that these ships might be attacked and captured by English and French privateers forced the Spanish government to set up a system of convoys to protect these ships from attack.

- This enabled Spain to pay for further expeditions to the New World and across the Pacific to places such as the Philippines, which also became part of the Spanish Empire.

- It also helped finance the expansion and equipment of the Spanish army. This enabled Spain to make war with France (1542–46) and established it as Europe's dominant military power by 1550.

- The discovery of silver was also important because it was used to make coins known as 'pieces of eight'. This allowed extensive trade with other countries in Europe, which made many Spanish merchants, and the government, very wealthy. However, longer term this meant that Spanish industry was neglected and it also led to inflation.

(ii) An answer about why Cortes's time as governor and captain-general of New Spain was important for the Aztecs might include these points:
- Cortes's reign as governor and captain-general of New Spain was important because it transformed the lives of the Aztecs. The capture of Tenochtitlan (1521) and the murder of the Aztec nobility and priests, as well as that of the Emperor Montezuma, meant that the Aztec ruling class was wiped out and ordinary Aztecs were required to accept Spanish rule.
- Cortes's reign was important because it led to major religious change. The Aztecs were required to give up their religion with its emphasis on fertility and human sacrifice and instead accept Christianity. This meant that they had to accept religious conversion and Christian baptism, while Aztec temples and shrines were replaced by Christian churches.
- Finally, the Aztecs also had to accept the *encomienda* system. This meant that they were required to work on the estates of Spanish settlers and conquistadors as well as paying tribute in the form of gold, silver, labour or maize. As a result, as Bartolome de las Casas noted, the Aztecs were often exploited by the Spanish.

(iii) An answer about why Pizarro's expedition of 1526–27 was important for the growth of the Spanish Empire might include these points:
- Pizarro's expedition of 1526–27 was important because it led to the discovery of the Inca Empire. Pizarro's early expeditions brought him directly into contact with the wealth of the Inca Empire, which was based in Peru and Bolivia.
- These discoveries led Pizarro to demand a further expedition to bring the Inca Empire and its wealth under Spanish control. Unable to gain the support of Pedro de los Rios, governor of Panama, Pizarro returned to Spain in 1528 and appealed directly to the Spanish king, Charles I, promising to 'extend the empire of Castile'.
- Charles granted a licence, the *Capitulacion de Toledo,* in July 1529. This meant that Pizarro had the authority to conquer Peru on behalf of Spain.
- The eventual success of Pizarro's expedition meant that, by 1540, the Spanish Empire had expanded, the Inca Empire had collapsed and most of its territory had been brought under Spanish control.

Notes

Notes

Notes

Notes

Notes

Published by Pearson Education Limited, 80 Strand, London, WC2R 0RL.

www.pearsonschoolsandfecolleges.co.uk

Copies of official specifications for all Pearson qualifications may be found on the website: qualifications.pearson.com

Text © Pearson Education Limited 2017
Produced by Out of House Publishing
Typeset and illustrated by Tech-Set Limited, Gateshead
Cover illustration by Kamae Design Ltd

The right of Brian Dowse to be identified as author of this work has been asserted by him in accordance with the Copyright, Designs and Patents Act 1988.

First published 2017

24
10 9 8 7

British Library Cataloguing in Publication Data
A catalogue record for this book is available from the British Library

ISBN 978 1 292 17644 4

Copyright notice
All rights reserved. No part of this publication may be reproduced in any form or by any means (including photocopying or storing it in any medium by electronic means and whether or not transiently or incidentally to some other use of this publication) without the written permission of the copyright owner, except in accordance with the provisions of the Copyright, Designs and Patents Act 1988 or under the terms of a licence issued by the Copyright Licensing Agency, 5th Floor, Shackleton House, Hay's Galleria, 4 Battle Bridge Lane, London, SE1 2HX (www.cla.co.uk). Applications for the copyright owner's written permission should be addressed to the publisher.

Printed in Great Britain by Bell and Bain Ltd, Glasgow

Acknowledgements
Content is included from Rob Bircher, Victoria Payne and Kirsty Taylor.

The author and publisher would like to thank the following individuals and organisations for permission to reproduce photographs:

Alamy Stock Photo: Granger Historical Picture Archive 9; Lanmas 11; The Granger Collection 14; Colport 15; The Granger Collection 16; Pictorial Press Ltd 19; Interfoto 20; Chronicle 22; Classicpaintings 24; Art Collection2 25; **Bridgeman Art Library:** Ms 604/1339 f.64v King Ferdinand II of Aragon and Isabella of Castile, from the 'Devotionary of Queen Juana the Mad, c.1482 (vellum), French School, (15th century) / Musee Conde, Chantilly, France 1; A Settlement on the Upper Pomeroon, Sambura, Guiana: Caribs Crushing Sugar Cane and Making Cassava Bread, from 'Indian Tribes of Guiana' (colour litho), Brett, W.H. (19th century) / Royal Geographical Society, London, UK 5; **Shutterstock:** Everett Art 2; Rook76 7

All other images © Pearson Education

Notes from the publisher
1. In order to ensure that this resource offers high-quality support for the associated Pearson qualification, it has been through a review process by the awarding body. This process confirms that this resource fully covers the teaching and learning content of the specification or part of a specification at which it is aimed. It also confirms that it demonstrates an appropriate balance between the development of subject skills, knowledge and understanding, in addition to preparation for assessment.

Endorsement does not cover any guidance on assessment activities or processes (e.g. practice questions or advice on how to answer assessment questions), included in the resource nor does it prescribe any particular approach to the teaching or delivery of a related course.

While the publishers have made every attempt to ensure that advice on the qualification and its assessment is accurate, the official specification and associated assessment guidance materials are the only authoritative source of information and should always be referred to for definitive guidance.

Pearson examiners have not contributed to any sections in this resource relevant to examination papers for which they have responsibility.

Examiners will not use endorsed resources as a source of material for any assessment set by Pearson.

Endorsement of a resource does not mean that the resource is required to achieve this Pearson qualification, nor does it mean that it is the only suitable material available to support the qualification, and any resource lists produced by the awarding body shall include this and other appropriate resources.

2. Pearson has robust editorial processes, including answer and fact checks, to ensure the accuracy of the content in this publication, and every effort is made to ensure this publication is free of errors. We are, however, only human, and occasionally errors do occur. Pearson is not liable for any misunderstandings that arise as a result of errors in this publication, but it is our priority to ensure that the content is accurate. If you spot an error, please do contact us at resourcescorrections@pearson.com so we can make sure it is corrected.